"Not your ordinary 'Dobsonesque' book about marriage, this is a relatable story about a man and a woman who believed their marriage was over, and only by a string of God's good grace did they have a chance of saving it. But that string of grace was more than enough, and Julie weaves it perfectly through her entire narrative."
—Matthew Paul Turner, author, *Christian Culture Survival Guide* and *Coffeehouse Gospel*

"Fidler writes with a poignant honesty. With self-awareness and humor, she confronts the difficulties and failures in her life and honors the passion and love that brought her and her husband together in the first place. This book will change your perspective on marriage—and it will encourage you to pursue your relationships with honesty and integrity."
—Renee Altson, author, *Stumbling Toward Faith*

"If you're looking for a book that avoids all of the fluffy, fairy tale dialogue that comes with so many Christian-based relationship books, this one is for you."
—Shellie R. Warren, author, *Inside of Me: Lessons of Lust, Love and Redemption*

"Julie Fidler's writing is both wincingly funny and brutally honest. By putting the magnifying glass so fully on herself, she exposes the issues at the heart of every marriage, that is, how each of us make it work through the best of times, and more importantly, through the worst of times. A great read that will surely be one of the most talked-about books of the year."
—Matt Bronleewe, songwriter/producer

For Better or the Absolute Worst

Adventures in Holy Matrimony

Julie Anne Fidler

[RELEVANTBOOKS]
WWW.RELEVANTBOOKS.COM

Published by Relevant Books
A division of Relevant Media Group, Inc.

www.relevantbooks.com
www.relevantmediagroup.com

© 2005 Relevant Media Group

Design by Relevant Solutions
Cover design by Mark Arnold
Interior design by Jeremy Kennedy

Library of Congress Control Number: 2005902179
International Standard Book Number: 0-9760357-9-0

For information or bulk orders:
RELEVANT MEDIA GROUP, INC.
100 SOUTH LAKE DESTINY DR. STE. 200
ORLANDO, FL 32810
407-660-1411

05 06 07 08 9 8 7 6 5 4 3 2 1

Printed in the United States of America

To Scott
My husband, lover, and best friend

Contents

Acknowledgments

Throughout my life, God has always put the right people in my life at exactly the right times, and that was certainly true when it came to writing this book. I can't list them all, but some people have to be thanked publicly.

To my amazing husband, Scott, who courageously swallowed his pride and gave me his blessing to write about the most intimate parts of our life together. I know it was not easy for him, but he believed as I did that our story would help people, and that was his primary motivation. I am blessed beyond measure to have such a wonderful man in my life, and I love him more than words can express. He is my heart.

To Shaunti Feldhahn, who put her (extremely busy) life on hold several times to come to my rescue, both personally and professionally. This wouldn't have been possible without her—literally. Words can't begin to express my gratitude, sister. You know why. Love you, friend.

To my family, who kept tabs on my progress and offered their assistance. They were excited for me and proud of me—albeit (understandably) a little nervous about the content of the book! I need to thank my parents especially, Gil and Barbara Smart, for raising me with the belief that families stick together no matter what. Their nearly forty-year marriage inspired me to work at my own.

To Mark and Jennifer Mayhue, our friends, prayer warriors, and accountability partners for a long time now, and we are still married, in large part, because of their love and support. Thank you, friends, for your honesty, vulnerability, and, of course, laughs!

To my supervisor Anne Redcay for being so flexible with my schedule, and to Tia Shaffer, Johanna Mayol, and Kelli Turgyan for listening to me ramble about all of this. Thanks also to Phil Hershey for his assistance.

To Cara Davis, Jeff Jackson, Cameron Strang and the rest of my new family at Relevant Books. You have all been so cool to work with. Thank you for believing in this book and in me as an author. You've made my lifelong dream a reality.

To Ben Wilson of Marriages Restored, whose friendship and expertise played a big role in the writing of this book.

To the hugely talented people I work alongside at *Infuze* magazine—editor Robin Parrish, Brian Palmer, Andy Paschen, Josh Hurst, Mark Knoles, Dana Lucas Timmerman, Paul A. Rose, Renee Altson and Matt Bronleewe. It is comforting to know you are at the ready with prayer, advice, and assistance. Special thanks to Renee and Matt—they know why!

ACKNOWLEDGMENTS

To Steve Seeber and Kathy Blankenbiller of The Lititz Record Express, who gave me some great opportunities, believed in me, and always made me feel like I was a part of something special. (Ad copy not included, of course!)

To Lancaster Evangelical Free Church, and especially to Pastor Doug Winne for his godly advice and counsel, as well as Phyllis Livsey and Diane Haenle for so graciously meeting our needs on a spiritual and practical level.

To the many, many friends who encouraged and prayed for me as I wrote this, and stuck by me when times were tough: Paul and Kathy Zubik, Steve and Patty Dietch (my "other family" for many years now), Dave and Lori Weidenhammer, Jon and Nancy Hawk, Greg Lowe and his lovely fiancée Cindy Borger, Juli Hong, Ginny Carlson, Susan McLaughlin, Susan Ribbeck, Jay and TJ Thompson, and Skip and Amanda Schoell, as well as everyone on my "prayer list," and the many readers who have encouraged me with their feedback over the years.

To my beautiful Savior who is responsible for blessing me with everyone I've listed here. You captured my heart when I was thirteen years old, and You never let go. You are my redeemer in so many ways. I pray this book glorifies You.

Foreword

By Shaunti Feldhahn

A few years ago, I got an email from a depressed young woman who had nearly given up hope on both her marriage and her life. She told me how much one of my novels had meant to her, speaking, as it did, about a young woman who found herself trapped in an unhealthy and desperate life path. As I read her words, I sensed something that had never happened before—I felt like the Lord was asking me to email her back in detail, to tell her how deeply He loved her and that He had amazing plans for her life.

That young woman was Julie Anne Fidler, and the book you hold in your hands is proof of the amazing power of God to transform a life and marriage—not just hers, but yours as well.

What began simply as an email conversation became, over the years, a deep and lasting friendship. In my friend, I see something that gives me great encouragement every day: someone who has had the deck stacked against her, has made some very poor life choices, and has suffered the consequences of both those choices and deep hurt caused by others—but who, despite it all, clings to God and is willing to endure the refining fire that brings transformation. And she does so with grace and humor. Most of the time.

At one point when I was talking to Julie's pastor, he confessed his surprise that she of all people was writing a marriage book. You see, Julie and her husband, Scott, have had plenty of problems. Theirs is not the white-picket-fence, glorious twenty-five-year relationship that characterizes the authors of most marriage books. Both Julie and Scott have had habits, dysfunctions, and histories that created serious cracks in their marital launching pad. As you will learn in these pages, Julie has struggled with deep wounds from her past, bipolar depression, and unhealthy relationship habits that built up for years before she got married. Not surprisingly, their marital union soon turned rocky, painful, tumultuous—until both parties thought surely it would be better to just give up.

The only thing Julie and Scott had going for them was that individually they were holding tightly to the only solid rock amidst the storm—Jesus Christ. They relied on that solid ground to fight the temptation to quit.

And that is exactly why Julie needs to write this book. In today's culture, hundreds of thousands of couples come to marriage each year with many of the same handicaps that Julie and Scott faced. And many have felt the same thing: no one understands; it'll never change; it would be far better to just divorce. And those couples need to hear the astounding truth: there is another way. A hard way, but a better way, of choosing to commit, sticking with it through the pain, and working through issues individually and together, until the marriage comes out of the darkness and into the light—and is that much richer and more precious for the work that has been done.

Julie is not looking back on their marriage troubles with the ease of distance. God chose her to write this book because she's been in it so recently – as recently as each individual chapter was being written. She learned many of the lessons you'll read here even as she was writing them down.

And it has been precious to see my friend, in the words of the hymn, "tempted, tried, and sometimes failing" but always deeply desiring to get back up and cling to God as her only hope. Always willing to not just blame others, but accept responsibility for her own actions and ask forgiveness, from her husband and from the Lord. And always willing to confront even the hard things with a sense of humor. I believe it will be so valuable for you, the reader, to walk close in Julie's footsteps, watching from only a short distance behind as she wrestles with both painful trials and life-giving opportunities.

I believe Julie's story will give you hope. She and her husband never thought they'd make it past year three. As you read this, they are on year five; their marriage is restored; and they are entering into a time of ministry to others who are—perhaps like you—just a few steps behind. They will need to remain ever vigilant, but they have seen the delight that comes from committing to each other and refusing to quit. You will, too.

Come along, and be encouraged.

SHAUNTI FELDHAHN
author, *For Women Only: What You Need to Know About the Inner Lives of Men*

Introduction

What Did You Expect?
(or What You Don't Expect)

What did you expect when you got married? Probably a few speed bumps, like learning how to work together as a team, figuring out how to get your spouse to stop snoring without smacking him with your pillow, and blending your personalities and backgrounds together in a way that both complements and works for you. You know, typical newlywed stuff!

What you don't expect in the first few years of your marriage is serious illness, multiple surgeries, job loss, financial ruin, or a lack of physical intimacy, just for starters. You always hope you won't see much of that over the course of your marriage, but it never really occurs to you that it could happen literally the day after your partner slips that wedding band on your finger. Having problems early on is more of a hurdle than having them, say, fifteen years down the road. Your high hopes and aspirations are assaulted by fear and disappointment. You exchange joy for anger, and if you don't know where to turn for help, anger can turn into bitterness, and that's how your union starts to crumble. In the midst of trying to learn how to cook and change a vacuum cleaner bag, my husband's health was deteriorating, and the bills were piling up.

I began to resent him, which made him resent me. There finally came a night last winter when we had to make a choice to either throw in the towel or fight for our marriage. We had gone out on a date that night, trying to rekindle the spark that once existed between us, but we were fighting as soon as we hit the road. We ate dinner in silence, and the tension in the car on the way home was unbearable. I finally turned to my husband and asked, "Do you want to get divorced?" He said he didn't know. Through tears, we discussed our options. Until that night, divorce was just something we kept in the back of our minds, not a realistic possibility, and being faced with it made us see we still had a little bit of fight left in us. We acknowledged that we were unhappy and that there was a huge schism between us, but we weren't ready to give up just yet. We wanted to make our marriage work, not because of warm, fuzzy feelings (we didn't have any of those left!) but because we believed it was the right thing to do. We agreed to set about the work necessary to improve things immediately.

Help was hard to come by, since we were dealing with atypical challenges. We scoured the bookstores for helpful reading material but found "white picket fence" books that covered most standard problems, but not many unique ones. Our saving grace was the center strand in our cord of three—God. Our only instruction guide was the Bible, but as we sought out God's counsel, He put the right people in our path to help us. Nobody had any easy answers for us. In fact, most people admitted upfront that they weren't at all used to dealing with situations like ours. But those people prayed for us, encouraged us, and wouldn't let us give up when it seemed the easiest thing in the world.

We both had a lot of work to do (and still do), and it wasn't easy. There were stops and starts, and sometimes I wondered if I would be better off living alone with nothing but a bunch of cats. At times I was so torn about what to do—many of my friends and some of my family members believed it would be easier on me if I just called it quits. But the results of the hard work, determination, and even the second-guessing were the beginnings of a healed marriage and a deeply cultivated love and friendship between my husband and me. Instead of learning our lessons through a blissful honeymoon period like most people, we learned our lessons the hardest way possible, over time. And make no mistake about it—it took a lot of stupidity to get us to where we are today!

As I began writing online about the struggles in my marriage, I started receiving emails from other young couples seeking advice. At the same time, a friend who had mentored me said she thought that eventually our experiences would be used to help others. In July 2004, I was approached about writing a book, and I knew almost immediately that marriage would be my topic.

This is not just a memoir or an entertaining look at the strange and unfortunate occurrences in the lives of two dense newlyweds living on love and creative variations of macaroni and cheese. As I said, I get emails all the time from people who are disappointed with their marriage. They are frustrated because the mushy feelings have faded, the fun has become infrequent, and the need for hard work and perseverance has never been more apparent. It hurts when your marriage is struggling—I know. And sometimes fighting for your union is the most painful thing you could ever do—far beyond the pain of a relationship that is standing still and rotting away. Standing up for your marriage requires you to open yourself up and be willing to confront your deepest wounds. The junk you've been ignoring becomes the very junk you have to sift through.

But I'm beginning to see how amazing the reward is. It's so worth the pain. I look at our marriage now, and I'm humbled that God miraculously reached into our relationship and began a process of healing, simply because (I believe) we made ourselves willing to go through it. We were at the end of our strength, and I'd almost completely given up hope, but God saved us. I believe—no, I *know*—He can do the same for anyone else. And that's the point of this whole book. I'll be the first to tell you that I am not a psychologist or a marriage counselor. I write out of personal experience, which is the greatest teacher of all. I wrote this out of my desire to share what is working for us with others. It's practical advice—stuff we never would have learned had we not had to stand on the front lines of battle ourselves. My hope is that this book will land in the hands of another young couple facing hardship, who need something besides well wishers and all the "white picket fence" books on the shelf. I hope this will be a unique tool to those facing unique challenges. I also hope it serves as an eye-opening education for bleary-eyed lovers who are engrossed in organizing seating arrangements and picking out china patterns.

You see, there were some pretty big lies the enemy fed us along the way, and we believed them. Why were we so prone to believe them? Because we fell into the trap of believing the first and perhaps biggest lie of all: *Our marriage was safe.* We believed a husband and wife should pray together, but mostly for intimacy reasons. We didn't give much thought to a couple praying together for actual protection, nor did we think much about getting others to pray for us, as well. It wasn't exactly that we disbelieved it; it's just that it honestly never crossed our minds. All I can do is slap my forehead in hindsight.

Through believing that first, harmful lie, we went on to believe a host of others, sometimes in unison as a couple, sometimes on our own. Opening that one window opened up all sorts of other doors. For example, I believed that I was a whole enough person to commit my life to someone else. Instead of feeling an urgency to confront my past—which included sexual abuse and years of depression because of it—I wrongly believed that getting married would fill in the empty places in my life and "heal" those wounds. I was so sold out to this lie; I didn't even realize I had bought into it until my marriage was truly on the verge of ending. I believed that my own painful past would not cast shadows on my marriage. I figured getting married symbolized growing up and moving beyond my wounds and mistakes.

Instead, old hurts caused new problems, and instead of being miraculously healed by marriage, I wound up creating new hurts instead—not just for me to heal from, but for my husband to heal from, too.

What I found in the painful interim between our darkest days and the true restoration of our relationship, as we were trying to figure out what should happen next, was that my marriage was based on a whole *host* of lies.

I watched helplessly as my husband's health slowly deteriorated, sapping him of his energy, and robbing us of a sexual relationship. And I—a young wife, fresh from her parents' home, in her early twenties, and totally clueless—went from being an enthusiastic new bride to a caretaker much of the time. The disappointment I felt took me to depths of sorrow I never dreamed I'd experience in the "honeymoon phase" of my marriage. Regret began to creep in, and my romantic feelings for my husband diminished. I thought that a lack of feelings meant a lack of love, and I didn't stop to consider that love is a choice.

Thank God for a friend's direction to do loving things even as I considered completely shutting down or running away. I had begun to think that if I didn't feel wildly romantic toward my husband, then nothing else was worth saving.

My husband and I believed the only way to handle the painful feelings of loss and disappointment that stemmed from the lack of a sexual relationship was to stop touching, holding, and nurturing each other completely—to simply snip the lines of physical communication and become like restless, platonic roommates. The truth is, even when sexual intercourse is an impossibility, there are other ways of being sensual, and couples can absolutely find fulfillment with a little patience and creativity. We couldn't hear these words whispered in our ears by the Father who put us together because our hearts were already turning to stone with resentment and unresolved grief. Only hitting rock bottom could shatter our hearts and make them pliable again.

We started out our marriage with plenty of money. We had an adorable home on Main Street in a Norman Rockwell-type town, two cars, great jobs, dreams of having children in the first year, and the naive belief that it would always stay that way. We didn't think we'd ever be totally broke and living on instant food and the mercy of others—we didn't bother to save any money!

We believed that fun should win out over responsibility in the early years, but this was a two-parter. We *also* believed that we were the only ones who were in debt and so poor that buying a pack of gum was a "treat."

And we struggled to come to terms with the highs and lows of my Bipolar Disorder, I was forced to face up to the fact that I had been trying to survive on my own, without the appropriate help. And in believing and living the lie that I was just fine by myself, I was becoming sicker, and my marriage was becoming more fragile.

So this is our story of overcoming those lies and defeating the ultimate liar of all.

Don't be fooled—he still fires shots at us, and sometimes we're too slow to duck. But we're wise to the game now.

My hope is that this book will help teach you some of the things we had to learn by nearly coming apart.

And I hope to provide a few laughs along the way.

Chapter One

Young and In Love ...
and Totally Naïve

If you were to ask any of my friends what has defined my young marriage thus far, they would probably say "chaos!" We are not your typical couple. I got the flu on our honeymoon, and a week later my husband had emergency double knee surgery. Frankly, I think that set the tone for our union for several years to come.

I had these grandiose dreams about marriage, which were not entirely unlike the dreams of any other young woman. I had my entire wedding planned out by the time I was twelve, right down to the flavor of the filling in the cake. (It was raspberry, and it was delicious.) Every love song on the radio evoked that first dance.

I have heard many girlfriends complain that their fiancés weren't particularly interested in the wedding plans. I must have lucked out big time, because my fiancé, Scott, was just as excited as I was. When I got stressed out, he took over. He showed the same concern over the flowers on the cake as he showed over his favorite football team's next big game—and that's saying a lot for the guy. I found my dress, and everything fell into place. The niece and nephew I was about to inherit agreed to be in the wedding party; the church was something out of a fairy tale; and most of my family members were coming in from New York for the big day. Definitely a dream come true. No reason to believe our marriage itself would be anything but!

That's the problem with most people, though, isn't it? They equate a beautiful wedding with a beautiful marriage. Sure, you can have a beautiful marriage, but it's not all wine and roses. I can't tell you how many people tried to warn us that it wasn't always going to be a dream come true. We just didn't want to listen. Anyone who told us anything other than what we wanted to hear was promptly shut out and dismissed as trying to ruin the great thing we had together. (Which wasn't giving our pals much credit, since none of them would ever purposely steer us wrong!)

We should have listened.

It turned out that married life was a trial by fire. We went from whispering sweet nothings into each other's ears at the reception to practically wringing each other's necks in the bedroom.

And you know what? It was necessary. It still hurts sometimes. We have so much learning to do. But we're fully committed to each other now—and in love with each other again—which is more than I can say about the state of our union a year ago. Duking it out and refusing to quit are exactly what saved us, and I believe that can save just about anyone who is willing to put up a good fight. Not a fight with each other, but a fight together against the many forces that conspired to divide us. And as you'll see in the coming pages, there were many, many potential divisions. Perhaps even some of the same ones—whether quirky or devastating—that are stalking your union right now.

In today's world, many people bring a lot of background brokenness to marriage. We sure did. I believe people need to see that even a man and woman who look good on the outside but are messed up on the inside—even people who have made some stupid, sinful choices—are able to overcome those stumbling blocks through the power of Jesus. During my many dark, dark days, I went to our local Christian bookstore looking for something—anything—that would walk me through my messed-up state and messed-up marriage. I found lots of marriage books—good books, many of them—but I just couldn't identify with the perfect, smiling couples on the cover. These books looked like the hardest thing the marriage counselor/authors had encountered was an argument over whether to get the Lexus or the Beemer. What would they know about the marital ramifications of bipolar depression? Pornography? Fatherlessness? Poverty? Sexual abuse?

I left the bookstore, feeling defeated. But we serve a great God. In the years to follow, God brought us something much better than a book. We were blessed with amazing friends who were willing to offer us painfully honest renditions of their own stories, and their successes—and their challenges to us—became our inspiration. That's why I believe none of our own struggles will be in vain. I'm trusting God that our stumbling blocks will be stepping stones for other searching couples.

Where We Come From

Perhaps like some of you, my husband didn't have a Beaver Cleaver-type of existence growing up. He comes from a broken home and never knew his biological father. His adoptive father

3

died when Scott was only three. My mother-in-law worked at a feverish pace to keep food on the table for Scott and his older brother, but sometimes there was no food. My husband can recall many nights of eating only cereal for dinner because there was nothing else in the cupboard. He grew up in poverty, yet he can look anyone in the eyes and tell him he had a wonderful, happy childhood.

He swears his mother never yelled at him. He says that when she was angry, she actually got quieter. For the most part, Gloria was a pretty docile woman, and Scott never felt threatened. He talks about midnight games of Tag with family and friends and time spent at the beach. The town he grew up in was very much "in the boonies." Everybody knew everybody else's business, and the nearest hospital was a good twenty miles away. Kids graduated from high school and got married or took a job in a local factory or grocery store. It was more likely that kids from my husband's side of town would get married young and never move out of the area than it was that they leave and go to college. I've always had this fascination with big cities and a desire to move to one. My husband looks at me like I'm growing antennae out of my forehead every time I bring it up.

Scott wasn't exactly a "player," either. He had a few girlfriends but nothing really serious. He was brought up to respect women and to be sensitive to their needs. So he never played the field or tried to score with as many chicks as possible. He wasn't about impressing his friends, and I believe him when he says this, because it takes a big man to admit to something like that. He didn't want to be intimate with someone he wasn't committed to for life, so when he came into my world at the ripe old age of twenty-seven, he was still a virgin, and I was utterly amazed that twenty-seven-year-old male virgins existed.

My life was considerably different growing up. I come from an intact family. My parents have been married for almost forty years. I have memories of my father taking me sledding in the winter around our area of Pennsylvania and then to a restaurant for hot chocolate with extra marshmallows. I spent summers at my grandparents' house in New York, hunting for seashells with my cousins at Jones Beach. My dad drove my mother crazy by standing in the middle of the front yard during thunderstorms. She'd stand at the screen door and scream at him, "Are you NUTS? Get in this house right now!" He'd light another cigarette and blow her off; when she was out of sight, he'd pull me out into the yard with him and tell me about the storm clouds casting a murky gray over the sky. It's amazing neither of us ever got struck by lightning.

I don't have a lot of happy memories, though. A lot of my childhood memories are sad. My parents had a lot on their plates when I was little. They were caring for one of my grandmothers, who had become senile and physically unable to take care of herself. One of my older brothers suffered from Cystic Acne, which caused temporary skin disfigurement, and that made him a target for bullying as a teenager. A number of other unfortunate circumstances had a grip on our family. Back then, we didn't talk about any of it. None of it had a name, but it set the tone in the house. An overall sadness permeated the air.

What really ruined those years for me, however, was the sexual molestation I endured at the hands of a neighbor. When people ask me how long it lasted, I can't give them an exact time frame. I don't know for sure, but it happened over the course of years. I can't be certain how old I was when it began, but in my earliest memory, I am three or four years old. I didn't ask for what happened to me. I don't know of anyone who would. But I never told anyone at the time. And as I grew, I never simply "ran away" from it because it filled a void. I grew up feeling very displaced, and the other kids seemed to value me about as much as they'd value a piece of garbage on the street. As disturbing as it is to admit it, I didn't run away because at least at his house, I was the focus of somebody's attention. As a result, even now in my late twenties, I'm still learning the difference between sex and love, as well as how they go together.

As a teenager, I was at total odds with my mother. I always knew my family loved me, but we didn't talk much. I was going through a lot of unresolved issues because of the sexual abuse, but my mother told me to "just forget it happened." She meant well, but I couldn't "just forget" something that so shaped me and defined my early years. I believe we all have a tendency to try to keep a lid on the things that hurt us. I don't fault her for that anymore.

We fought ferociously, sometimes to the point of throwing furniture at each other. I said, "I hate you," more times than I could count, even though I never meant it deep down. My mother didn't understand me, and I didn't want her to. My mom had her own issues to deal with, but she was so focused on the people she had to take care of that she neglected herself. I didn't understand that as a kid, and I held it against her.

Like many abuse victims, I was ashamed of myself, of the abuse, of the struggles I was going through. I wanted her to love me and accept me so desperately, but I knew she could never grasp the things I felt inside. I preferred that we keep our distance from one another.

It was a lonely time in my life, so I did the only thing I could think to do—I acted out. I tried to kill myself, but I didn't want to die. I wanted someone to understand the level of sadness and desperation I had reached. I wanted somebody to love me and give me permission to feel hurt and violated. I also started cutting myself. I carried a box cutter in my backpack, and when I felt especially stressed or sad, I cut my arms and legs. It was somehow strangely relieving, yet I can say in all honesty that I did that for attention, too.

There was one light that came into the midst of my blackness during those years. I accepted Jesus as my Savior when I was thirteen. It was an earth-shaking experience. I felt genuinely changed and renewed. But I have come to believe that the true Christian life requires bringing the darkness to light. As hard as we try to keep things covered up, God is constantly seeking to let everything be known. Even though I was just a kid, I gave my heart to Him with pure expectations, but I was still gripped by fears and sorrows and unhealthy behaviors that felt all too natural to me. God was trying to pull back the curtain, but I slapped His hand away and chose not to trust. I was just a kid.

And there was the sex thing, too. Sex was love, and love was sex. The two were not just connected—they were virtually the same thing. I did a lot of things I'm not proud of. While attending a youth group retreat in high school, one of the speakers said, "Imagine your soul is like a daisy, and every time you have sex with someone outside of marriage, you're ripping one of the petals off. Eventually, you'll have to rip the leaves off too, until you're nothing but a stem. That's what premarital sex does to you." That was an accurate, heart-wrenching description. I gave a lot away during my teen years. Purity is easy to lose, and healing can be hard to come by. I'm thankful that we serve a God who makes all things new, in spite of imperfect fools like me. When I was intimate with somebody, I felt crushing shame; but if I wasn't intimate with somebody, I felt unlovable. Strangely enough, as I would come to find out, I wasn't being "intimate" with anybody. I was engaging in the cheap, rip-off version of intimacy, trading truth for lies.

I guess it's pretty obvious by now that Scott and I both entered into holy matrimony with enough baggage to weigh down a commuter jet. Especially on my side of the plane.

From Zero to One Hundred in Sixty Days

Scott and I started seeing each other in January 1999. We made our little romance official on Valentine's Day. By March, we were looking at rings. His friends were ecstatic. My friends wanted to have my head examined. And I don't blame them, looking back on it now.

In their defense, I suppose I did seem pretty irrational. I had gone away to college in Nashville, Tennessee. I wanted to be a song-writer, and my parents wouldn't agree to let me just move down there for a year or two. The only way to move there right away was to do so under the guise of pursuing an education. I didn't care about my education. I didn't think I needed it. So when I gave up on pursuing my education, nobody was surprised. That was how I worked back then—if it wasn't interesting to me, I didn't bother with it. (This is just one of the lovely patterns I was going to have to break to make my marriage work.)

I moved back to Pennsylvania and in with my parents, who were none too pleased to have me there. My mother stood in my doorway on the day I flew home and said, "If you think you're going to sit on your butt and do nothing, you've got another thing coming. You go in there first thing tomorrow and tell your boss you need full-time work." So I went back to the nursing home where I had worked part-time in high school, and I groveled, and I got full-time work. I shocked my parents by turning into a complete and utter workaholic. I not only worked my normal hours, but I picked up extra shifts and helped coordinate special functions. I didn't like my job, but I was earning loads of money, and that was all I was concerned with. I had no expenses, apart from a small student loan. I told everybody that I would move back to Nashville permanently by the following summer. There was something kind of romantic about the whole idea.

All I did in my spare time was write songs. I was obsessed with my music. Through a friend at work, I met a guy named Brian, who was also a wannabe songwriter. He played the guitar too, and we had good chemistry, artistically. I worked all day, went drinking at night, and jammed with Brian into the wee hours of the morning. I spent a lot of time feeling really hung over. When I left Nashville, I didn't know what, if anything, I be-lieved about God anymore (ironically, this was partly due to attending a conservative Christian school there). On top of all this, I began to spiral into a deep depression, partly fueled by my dark lifestyle of running from God and partly by an as-yet-un-diagnosed clinical condition. I pulled further and further away from God the longer things went unaddressed.

That's the state I was in when Scott met me—depressed, drink-ing way too much, light-years away from God, and completely self-absorbed.

My friends knew how much my music meant to me. Most of them weren't Christians, so they didn't see a big issue with my alcohol consumption, but they were concerned about my depression, which I had dealt with all through high school, too. They thought that moving back to Tennessee would be good for me since I missed the city and my college friends so desperately. And I seemed determined and driven to make a go of the songwriting. I had made a lot of great connections and had a number of opportunities on my plate. All I had to do was move back to Nashville.

I remember the look on my best friend's face when I told her I was getting married. It was shock and horror, followed by hysterical laughter. Juli didn't like Scott anyway. It was nothing he did wrong; she just knew my track record with guys. I picked jerks who treated me poorly, and she was constantly on the defensive, on my behalf. She eventually grew to love Scott, but that didn't mean she was on board with the idea of me becoming his wife. It seemed to her like I was abandoning the dream I had had since I was twelve years old, when we used to worship the ground Amy Grant walked on. Not to mention the fact that I was so young, and she had hoped that I would finish my degree first. We argued over dinner at a local eatery, and I, of course, told her she was crazy and that I knew exactly what I was doing. After all, I told her, Scott would move back to Nashville with me after we got married ...

Scott and I were barely together for three months when we had "The Nashville Discussion." Scott said he loved me, but he didn't like the idea of having a wife who would be constantly traveling. Also, his family was here in Pennsylvania. His friends were here, and his job was here ... everything he had ever known was here. He didn't understand why I couldn't pursue my career from home.

But, really, he did understand. He was a music buyer before we met and had spent quite a bit of time in Nashville, dealing with record and distribution companies. He knew the ins and outs as well as I did. It was almost a given—in order to be successful, you had to be at the center of the action. And we both knew the action wasn't always healthy. Scott was more concerned with the ties that bind, and those ties were firmly knotted in central Pennsylvania. He said, without really saying it, that I had to decide what I wanted more, because I couldn't have both.

I loved him, and I couldn't imagine living my life without him. I wanted to commit my life to him and have children with him. So I fell into the all-too-familiar trap of believing, as many women do, that I could change his mind. I figured once we tied the knot, I'd be able to convince him to pack up and set our circus down eight hundred miles away. I didn't believe for a minute that I was trading in one dream for another. I was just adding an extension onto the original dream. So we forged ahead with the engagement ring and eventual wedding plans, all the while dodging phone calls from friends pleading with me to reconsider.

I would never advise anyone to get married as young as I did. Scott was older and much more settled; I was at an age that is normally reserved for acting crazy and not being tied down to anything, including a spouse. I was so immature, but I didn't realize it. That's what my friends tried to tell me, but I ignored them. They thought I should enjoy my youth, and I thought they needed to grow up.

Despite it all, the wedding was going to go on.

Charles Manson or Marriage Material?

Like a lot of techno-savvy people our age, Scott and I met

online. I was nineteen years old, had dated a succession of jerks, and was recovering from a breakup with yet another one of them. I was typing away, happily minding my own business, when I received an Instant Message from a complete stranger. He said he "liked my profile" and wanted to know if I was interested in chatting. For the the readers who aren't knowledgeable about the Internet, let me fill you in. Just because the electronic person you're chatting with says he is a 6'0" male, muscular, and a successful trial attorney, does not mean he really is any of those things. He could just as likely be a 5'2", overweight mortician with a really bad comb-over. Or, if you're really unlucky, he could be a serial killer. There's no way you can tell, so these are the chances you take.

I was a little nervous that I might be talking to a freak. But I was also bored, and it wasn't like I was giving him my address and Social Security number, so I humored him. That was in 1998, and we continued to chat for the better part of a year. I was so gun-shy from my past romantic failures; I made it clear I had no interest in a serious relationship—or at least that's what I told him and what I tried to convince myself of.

One day he asked me to meet him for dinner, and I panicked. I said we should talk on the phone first, so I called him up. It was the most boring conversation I'd ever had. I asked him a lot of really pointed questions: What is your favorite movie? How long have you been a Christian? What is your biggest struggle in life? And he answered all of my questions with a monotone, one-word answer. When he invited me out on a "mini-date," I felt obligated to say yes, just because I feared sounding rude. I figured we'd sit together in awkward silence over platefuls of pasta, go our separate ways, and be done with it.

The incredibly boring phone personality was great company

live and in living color. His insanity rivaled my own. He liked to have fun, and he had a twisted sense of humor—score. We shared a basket of bacon-onion-cheese fries and spent hours making the waitresses crazy, wishing we'd finish up and move on. There was so much to talk about, and we had so many interests in common. Scott is the kind of guy who holds the door open for you, pulls out your chair, asks if there's anything you need, and grabs the waitress's attention when you're out of Coke. Call me crazy, but I like that. I'd make a horrible feminist, wouldn't I? Anyway, I've never been a big believer in love at first sight, but I knew I was going to be spending a lot more time with this guy.

It was at a Super Bowl party a week later that I realized he might be marriage material. He introduced me to his throng of friends, and I munched on nachos while pretending to understand football. Since Scott is eight years older than me, many of his friends were already married with children. It became obvious within the first fifteen minutes that he was a kid magnet. He was the only person in the room who was willing to pry himself away from the game to entertain the children at the party (and I now understand what a sacrifice that is for him). I saw serious father potential—something really special. A lot of men would rather have their fingernails ripped off than roll around on the floor with their friends' kids.

I felt a lot of pressure that night to figure out where this new relationship was going. Would it be a good friendship, or something more? The party was held at the theological seminary where his best buddy was attending school, and during halftime Scott pulled me aside and showed me around campus. Alone in the chapel, he asked me what I thought.

"What do I think about what?" I asked him.

"Everything." He said. "What do you think about us?"

It was too early for me to tell whether or not we had a future together, and I didn't want him to get the wrong idea in case it didn't work out. I didn't want to seem like I was leading him on, but I had to admit ... I saw a future. As my mother always tells people, there's nothing not to like about my Scott. He's just a nice guy, and everybody loves him as soon as they meet him. I take a lot of pride in saying that. But a nice guy does not a husband make.

There was another interesting thing that happened that night, too. His pals were—probably rightly so—concerned about my spiritual status, partly because I had a smoking addiction at the time. One of them took me aside and told me that Scott's friends had been praying that he would find a wife. They all felt like he had so much to offer a woman, and as he approached thirty, his search for love sort of became everyone else's mission, too. I leaned against the counter in the kitchen with folded arms, listening politely as Jon ticked off all of Scott's good qualities on his fingers. Either they were sick of him and trying to get him out of their hair, or they were genuinely on a mission to "talk up" their friend in an effort to help him find a good woman. But they also wanted me to know that they were watching.

Scott asked me out to dinner later that same week, and I said yes. We became inseparable. We started cultivating love.

I was nineteen.

She Who Pays the Bill Gets the Last Word

I love my mother to death. Many of the things that used to
drive me nuts about her when I was growing up have becoming amusing quirks that give me a good laugh now, but I didn't
always feel that way. My mother would have made a great corporate executive. She rules with an iron fist, and what she says
goes. She takes flack from no one. Such a personality was very
useful when I was a teenager and needed somebody to get me
out of trouble at school, but when it came to planning my wedding, we constantly butted heads.

My mom comes from a wealthy family. She had the ultimate
fairy tale wedding and the reception was held at a posh New
York country club. Good news for her, bad news for me. Mom
had certain ideas about my wedding. I'm guessing she had these
ideas long before I was even born. She wanted me to have the
kind of wedding the New York relatives would talk about on
the four hour drive home, yet she didn't want to break the
bank. If we had grilled up roadkill and had a square dance for
our wedding reception, my father wouldn't have cared. In fact,
he would have been grateful that we were saving him money.
But my mom had it all planned out, and we didn't have much
room to argue since, after all, she was paying for it.

In a perfect world, I would have worn my mother's wedding
dress. It was a gorgeous dress, but my mom is about four inches
shorter than I am and much thinner, and there was no seamstress
on this earth who could make that happen. We decided I would
wear her headpiece, and we began shopping for the dress.

Mom used to do some modeling, and she is forever telling
me I'd be so beautiful if only I'd lose some weight. She means
well, but it is forever a bone of contention between us. I have
always said the perfect Christmas gift would be breast reduction

surgery, so it was horrifying having to ask my mother to literally stuff my cleavage into those dresses, only to have her poke the side of one of my boobs and say, "I bet that would go away if you lost a little weight."

I had my preferences. No ruffles, nothing puffy, no hoop skirts, nothing sleeveless, and the less cleavage, the better. And don't even think about sequins. If it had been up to me, I would have marched down the aisle in jeans and Nikes. I bet that would have given the New York relatives plenty to talk about on the drive home. But that wasn't to be, and in the end, it was my mom who picked out the dress I wore down the aisle. And it was beautiful. I've got to give credit where credit is due.

Scott and I chose October 28, 2000, as our wedding date—a fall wedding. No ice to contend with, but no groomsmen roasting in their tuxedos, either. We loved the idea of having falling leaves as the backdrop to our special day. And when we got back from our honeymoon, the holiday season would be upon us. So we decided on floating autumn-colored candles as the centerpieces at the reception.

My mother nearly dropped dead over the concept of having an orange candle on the table at a classy event. We were informed that we would be having floral centerpieces. Some of our already-married friends suggested various deejays, but my mother wanted a live band. We didn't want a live band. We told my mother we would be checking out a few deejays, but the live band thing was definitely out. No more than two days later, my mother came home from work with a name and a phone number and informed us that this would be our deejay. Defeated, we pulled out every CD we owned and made up a very detailed list in an effort to avoid as much disco as possible.

As the days counted down, we struggled mightily with purity. We succeeded at behaving ourselves for a little while, but then, we messed up. I was coming out of an unsettled, unholy life-style, but I wanted to have a godly relationship. I wanted to start over, settle down, be a good Christian woman, and eventually a holy wife. But we just couldn't keep our hands off each other. Years later, as I began to pursue healing and wholeness, our de-cision to have premarital sex would come back to haunt us, but I'll save that for another chapter.

My mother, who remained a virgin until her wedding night, was absolutely paranoid that I was having sex with Scott. She interrogated me every chance she got and lectured me about the importance of waiting. She nearly drove me crazy. I was al-ways telling her to back off and mind her own business. Wheth-er she realized it or not, my mother was my conscience. She intensified the feelings of guilt that I already had, so I brushed her off—but only because I knew she was right.

I knew then—and even more now—that in reality we were making a huge mistake. The culture—and some of my friends—wanted us to believe it was okay, but God told us otherwise. My mother had great wisdom in this area, and we would have been wise to heed her advice.

Maybe I'll drive my own daughter crazy someday, lecturing her about saving herself for marriage. But who knows—maybe I'll plant a seed that grows real purity in her, too.

I'm grateful my own mom at least tried.

The Special Day That Started Out a Nightmare

The night of our rehearsal, I was a wreck. Reality was hitting me hard. At the time, "Butterfly Kisses" was a popular song, so we jumped on the bandwagon and told the deejay that I wanted to dance to it with my dad. Like any popular song, it seemed to come on the radio about every five minutes. That meant I was bursting into tears every five minutes, too. I frequently asked Scott if he thought I was crazy, and he humored me by saying no. I had nightmares about tripping on my way down the aisle, landing face first in a pile of rose petals thrown by Scott's six-year-old niece.

The guy who married us, Pastor Mick, was a wonderful friend. He could sense I was a nut about to crack, so at the rehearsal he did his best to break the ice. He put on a Rastafarian wig and told me to relax in a Jamaican accent. On the first run-through, I nearly sprinted down the aisle. I started to cry when we were rehearsing our vows. I spent large amounts of time in the bathroom.

I was up late that night, getting the last of the favors ready, making sure I was packed for my honeymoon, trying to make sense of what I was about to do. In the hours just before my wedding, my heart raced, and I began to realize that I wasn't just starting a new life but saying goodbye to my old one. It was sad in its own way. I didn't belong to my parents anymore. I was about to be responsible for making another person happy, not just myself. I was about to become my parents, and I was about to face everything that scared the heck out of me when I was a teenager. I couldn't wait to take those vows and fall into my new spouse's arms, but part of me wished that I could curl up under the blankets and be Mommy and Daddy's forever.

I woke up bright and early on the morning of October 28. It was a sunny day, and windy. I didn't want to wake anybody else up, so I just threw on some clothes and drove to the salon. While I was there, I ran into a woman I used to work with who was actually coming to my wedding later in the day. She told me about the photographer who did her granddaughter's wedding and how awful she was. She said her granddaughter was suing her for losing two rolls of film and never refunding her money. I asked this woman for the photographer's name and nearly fell out of my salon chair when it turned out to be the same photographer we had hired.

Thankfully, I was with the same woman who had been doing my hair for years. I managed to calm myself down and enjoy my morning. I felt like a princess, which is no small feat for a life-long tomboy like me. When it was all over, I got out of my chair in a button-down denim shirt, a pair of sweatpants and flip-flops with a huge bridal headpiece stuck to my hair. I whipped out my debit card and looked around the salon as she swiped it through the reader.

"Uh, your card was declined." She ran it a second time, but it rejected the card again.

"What?" I grabbed the card out of her hand and dialed the eight hundred number on the back on a pay phone.

I was several hundred dollars in the negative. I was so stunned and upset that I nearly swallowed the receiver. I promised the stylist that I would be back to pay her in full and raced across the street to my bank, where I nearly tackled the first bank teller I saw and breathlessly told her of my dilemma, frantically waving the card in front of her face. She looked up my account and shook her head. There was no mistake. I was really broke! I forced myself not to cry. That money had been set aside for our honeymoon; we weren't going to have to worry about anything!

She printed out a statement, and I saw that I had been charged numerous times for the candy we bought for the reception. The card reader had been malfunctioning that day, so the cashier had swiped my card over and over, reassuring me that it wasn't going through and I didn't have to worry about it repeatedly charging me. But they obviously didn't know what they were talking about, and I wound up paying for the same candy order a dozen times. Sadly for me, it was a Saturday, and there was nothing they could do about it right then and there. Plus, they said they could probably only refund about half of it to me.

There I was, dressed like a hobo about to be married, and I was so angry I was shaking, but I couldn't remedy the situation.

When I stumbled through the door to my parents' home, my mother was in her robe, making coffee in the kitchen. She got a huge smile on her face and told me how wonderful my hair looked. I threw my purse across the room and burst into tears. She came running as I sat down in the middle of the living room floor and sobbed. I stuttered and stammered and told her about my debit card and the crackpot photographer. She assured me that my photographer was reputable (she was a friend of my mom's friend) and told me I would probably get a lot of monetary gifts (in addition to her own), so I shouldn't worry about being broke on the honeymoon. I calmed down and put eye drops in my bloodshot eyes. For all the hassles and arguments we had gone through over those last few months, my mom became my emotional support that day. She took good care of me and saw to it that I worried about nothing.

As she sat there rubbing my shoulders, I realized that all of her suggestions (and even demands) were not an effort to undermine me. They were her way of making sure I had the most beautiful wedding day possible. She had a fairy-tale wedding, and she wanted the same thing for me. On that day, the hassles were over. The big event had arrived, and the arguments stopped. She saw to it that I had everything I needed. She handled the stressors and coordinated everybody, so all I had to do was look pretty and show up. My mom was a great mom that day.

I'm old-fashioned about some things. I didn't want to see Scott on our wedding day until the doors opened and my father walked me down the aisle. But I snuck in a two-minute phone call to him that morning. He was so terrified that he could barely talk. I told him I loved him and that in just a few hours, we'd be one.

I told him to take an antacid and sit down, too.

Let's Tie the Knot Already!

I sat in the back of my parents' car on the way up to the church, and my mother periodically made eye contact with me in the rearview mirror.

"You okay?" she'd ask.

"Just thinking happy thoughts." I'd smile back.

It was a sea of chaos as soon as I walked into the church, but as I mentioned, my mother became Barbara the Chaos Slayer. She arranged the little bottles of bubbles on the table leading out the door, and she made sure the bows were firmly attached to the pews. Juli, the friend who had told me I was crazy for getting married in the first place, was my maid of honor, and she also took on the job of ridding my life of stress. As we got ready, I stood in the mirror, gawking at the sight of myself in a wedding gown. I had seen myself dressed up like that dozens of times before, at fittings and getting my pictures taken for the paper, but this time it was different. I began to get sentimental and teary. The emotion of that moment was shattered by my bridesmaid, Sue, running past me in her dress, with a bottle of cover-up makeup in her hand, frantically asking if someone would please try to cover the huge tattoo she had gotten on her back in college.

Perhaps the cutest part of my wedding day was Scott's six-year-old niece, Alex, who was our flower girl. She had a little white dress on, and her hair was full of curls. She was my little shadow the entire day. When somebody fixed my hair or adjusted my headpiece, Alex stood next to me, looking up at me in awe. Everywhere I went, she followed, holding my hand. My wedding dress had long, whispery, sheer sleeves that she loved to feel. We went over the plan. I handed her the basket filled with rose petals and made sure she understood that she was supposed to sprinkle them down the aisle as she walked, not throw them in heaps. She nodded in agreement. I told her to walk slowly. She looked up at the strange adults in the room and sheepishly nodded her head. You know what? She didn't sprinkle one single rose petal because she was so nervous but she made up for it by being absolutely adorable.

Everybody gets skittish at a wedding. Even the people in the bridal party—or, as I like to call them, the pit crew—get wound up and nervous. By the time the music started, Scott's niece and nephew were leaping all over the place, my bridesmaids were pacing, Pastor Mick was playing the air guitar (don't ask), and my mother was asking me every fifteen seconds if I felt okay. Much to everyone's dismay, the chapel was on the second floor, which meant Juli had to hold my train and follow me blindly up the stairs. I started walking, heard a thud, and realized I couldn't go any farther. I looked back and Juli was lying flat on her face on the stairs, still holding my train.

"Shut up and walk," she told me as I tried desperately to stifle my giggles.

My father took my arm, and we stood in front of the huge wooden doors, waiting for our cue. He told me not to put my veil over my face, because he was afraid he wouldn't be able to lift it properly. I don't remember what else we talked about, waiting for our lives to change. Everything was a blur, and the world seemed to come to a screeching halt.

Now, I've been to some weddings where the bride looked very serious, as though her face was going to crack, but most break into a huge, glorious smile as soon as they appear in that doorway. It must be uncontrollable, because I did the exact same thing. I caught one glimpse of my Scott at the end of the aisle, and I couldn't stop the joy bubbling up inside. I didn't care about falling on my face, or catching my sleeve on fire while trying to light our unity candle. I had one goal in mind: getting to Scott.

When my father and I arrived at the altar, he kissed my cheek and let me go off to a whole new world.

Scott didn't look nearly as thrilled. In fact, I was expecting him to keel over onto his groomsmen and cause a domino effect. He didn't smile; he didn't blink; he just stared at me while Greg, his best man, kept one hand on his shoulder at all times. I gave him a huge smile. He wobbled and winced but didn't return the sentiment. I didn't see him smile until we couldn't get the unity candle lit, and we couldn't help but laugh. Later on, when the ceremony was over and we were waiting for the receiving line to begin, I asked him why he looked like he was on the verge of death. Had he eaten a spoiled appetizer at the rehearsal dinner? No, he told me. His overwhelming shyness got the best of him, and when he saw the number of people in the church, he got scared.

Pastor Mick, who had done his very best to keep things lighthearted and humorous, talked a little bit about our friendship and the things we had been through together. The great thing about Mick is his transparency. He wasn't concerned with impressing people or putting up a front. He was as honest as a person could be and always willing to share his own struggles and shortcomings with us. We loved Mick, and in addition to his transparency, we loved his twisted sense of humor. But like mine, sometimes his humor came out at the wrong times. We were just a bit horrified when Mick held up a thick piece of three-ply white rope.

"I have a unique wedding gift for you," he said, grinning at us from his pulpit. "It's not your average gift, like a blender or a lamp. You'll probably get ten blenders today, by the way. No, this rope symbolizes your union with each other and with Christ. The Bible says a cord of three strands is not easily broken. I want you to hang this somewhere in your home, so you always remember that with God in the center of your relationship, that cord will never be broken." He handed us the piece of rope. We sniffed and each wiped away a rogue tear.

Mick leaned over, grinned once more, and said, "It's not for you to tie each other up with!"

Partying Like It's 1999

The deejay, who showed up driving a hearse, was set up at the reception hall with his collection of disco hits. The cake showed up in one piece, with none of the icing flowers smashed. The champagne was on the table, and Scott and I couldn't stop disappearing around the corner to smooch. Most married people can relate to the almost compulsive need to look at their hands right after saying "I do," to see if that wedding ring is really there. There was a lot of kissing, clinking of glasses, and hand staring.

There would have been more dancing ... had our friends not gotten lost on the way to the reception. Mark and Jen were the official keepers of the CDs, but as the limo pulled away and the guests began leaving the church, Jen had to use the restroom. When she came out, everyone was gone. Both of them were from out of town, so they didn't know how to get to the reception. As we frantically searched for them all over the reception hall, they were in the parking lot of the church, hoping someone would find them. They were eventually recovered by a fellow wedding guest who went on the hunt.

By the time Mark and Jen were recovered and brought back to the reception, we'd had our fill of disco. But if you're giddy enough, even disco sounds good. Our photographer was wandering around the building and missed our first slow dance as a couple so she made the deejay restart our music, which meant restarting our dance, so she could jam her huge camera in our faces and capture the pseudo-moment. At the height of the festivities, she disappeared into a back room with him, where they sat at a table, drinking. By the end of the night, the deejay was dead on his feet, and the photographer could barely walk.

The last song of the night was "Unchained Melody," and my husband was with a group of his buddies, talking. I grabbed his arm and said, "I want to dance with you." I don't know what was so magical about that. It was a pretty straightforward sentence, not in the least bit flowery. But Scott remembers it being incredibly romantic, and to this day, whenever that song comes on the radio, he smiles at me and asks me if I remember ...

Some of our friends gathered around us and prayed over us before we left for our hotel. We soaked in their prayers, fully and foolishly believing that life would be easy and carefree. Every night would be like our wedding reception. We'd do lots of slow dancing, and we would always feel that passionate about each other. Our friends prayed that our relationship would grow deeper and more intimate, that we might overcome the obstacles and painful circumstances that were sure to come our way.

But we didn't really believe that we'd confront any. At least, nothing serious. We said we understood that marriage was hard and that it required compromise and perseverance, but we didn't understand the depth of what that meant. We figured compromise and perseverance meant an argument every now and then. We had no idea what was headed our way, and I'm glad we didn't know. I think if we had known, we might have stood each other up at the altar!

It was very late when we got to our hotel. It was the hugest hotel room I'd ever seen, complete with its own wine cellar. We poured ourselves some wine and hopped up on the bed. Oh, God, I thought, this is the most comfortable bed I've ever felt in my life. I just wanted to pull the blankets over my head and go to sleep. I was exhausted. I hadn't had any real sleep in over a week, and now I was expected to have sex. We might have been more enthusiastic about it had we waited to have sex in the first place. But it was "old hat" to us and not particularly thrilling. It was a lesson we had to learn the hard way—God makes rules in order to protect us, that we "might have abundant life." We broke His rules, and it made that night, in particular, less abundant.

Still, even if you have a less-than-thrilling wedding night experience, you blow it off and assume that the rest of your life together will be glorious. The next morning, my husband and I sat with our families at my parents' home, where they had brunch for us, and we opened our gifts. We were blessed with more than enough money to get by, which eased my mind about the debit card fiasco. We kissed our families goodbye and left for the Finger Lakes in New York, where we had rented a cottage for ten days.

It was on our first vacation as a married couple that reality would slowly begin to seep in.

I Spent Our Entire Honeymoon in Bed ...

It was cold and windy in upstate New York. The combination of cold weather and my extremely weak immune system won out within twenty-four hours. As Scott and I sat across from each other at dinner, I realized my throat was beginning to get sore. I spent the next day—and five days after that—in bed with the flu. I tried to get up and feign enthusiasm for our honeymoon, but I couldn't breathe. Everything hurt, and I was so dizzy I had to steady myself by holding onto the kitchen counter. We got in the car and drove to a few wineries, but once we got there, I was either asleep or too dazed and achy to get out of the car and go on the tour. It was then that I learned what kind of man I had married.

I'll be blunt—if Scott had gotten the flu, and not me, I don't know how I would have reacted. My family has always had a "just deal with it," approach to illness. Faced with a sick husband on my honeymoon, I might have even been a little ticked off, even though it wouldn't have been his fault. I know I would have been disappointed, and I'm sure Scott was disappointed. But he never told me, not even once. He took care of me, made me tea, made sure I had something to eat, rubbed my back, and told me he loved me. He didn't complain, even as I sat on the couch, looking like death was at my doorstep, watching *Jerry Springer* on what was supposed to be the most romantic week of our lives.

"I have the rest of my life to love you," he told me, "and I can wait a few days for it to start."

By the end of the trip, I was feeling better, and we did have fun. We spent a day driving through the countryside and went to Niagra Falls, where we ate dinner on the Canadian side. We went out to dinner at beautiful restaurants, and finally toured a few of those wineries where I'd almost slipped into a coma earlier in the week. We enjoyed the last few days of our trip and managed to cram a lot of activity into a very short span of time.

We also decided to take another stab at sex. It seemed odd, that after months of Scott not being able to keep his hands off me, he was not approaching me for sex now that I was over the flu. I approached him, not unlike I would have approached him before we got married. He was a willing participant, but he seemed disinterested. And there were problems, too. He wasn't functioning the way a guy should function. I was concerned, but not really worried. I chalked his problems up to the same thing that caused me to come down with the flu—weird weather and not enough sleep. But Scott was mortified, as I've come to learn all men are when they "can't get it up," and apologized profusely. I told him not to worry about it, and I really meant it.

There would be plenty of time for that.

There would be plenty of time to make up for the honeymoon that didn't live up to our expectations.

When we got home, that's when the real fun would begin.

But even though I wasn't overly concerned with his physical problems, I was disappointed. There were no two ways about it—one of my romantic dreams (admittedly sex-filled) was dashed on our honeymoon. And apart from the sexual issues, something else was weighing me down. I had an uneasy, gnawing feeling in the pit of my stomach. It was the same feeling I got when I was in denial about something, usually that I was dating a jerk. In fact, one of the reasons I knew Scott was "the one" was because of my lack of uneasy feelings early on in our relationship.

I took the gnawing feeling to mean that I had made a mistake in getting married, and it didn't go away for a good six months. As I would eventually come to realize, it was not an indication that I had made a bad choice in getting married, but that I had made a bad choice in getting married with so much unresolved stuff from the past. The gnawing would eventually evolve into chronic stomach problems.

I went into the first days, weeks, and months of married life feeling conflicted and alone.

It was a recipe for deep depression.

It almost wiped my world away.

Reflections

1. What are/were your expectations of marriage?

2. Does your idea of marriage match up with the things you were taught growing up? Have you been pleasantly surprised, or disappointed?

3. What kinds of marriages did you observe growing up?

4. What one thing do you wish you had done differently in the earliest days of your marriage?

5. What did you do right?

Scriptures:

Hebrews 13:4
Marriage should be honored by all, and the marriage bed kept pure, for God will judge the adulterer and all the sexually immoral.

Isaiah 33:6
He will be the sure foundation for your times, a rich store of salvation and wisdom and knowledge; the fear of the LORD is the key to this treasure.

Psalm 127:1
Unless the LORD builds the house, its builders labor in vain. Unless the LORD watches over the city, the watchmen stand guard in vain.

Chapter Two

Living Down
a Painful Past

I have this long-running joke with my husband that when he started dating me, he was woefully unequally yoked. There he was, this athletic twenty-seven-year-old man who was ready to settle down with a nice, godly woman who enjoyed the simpler things in life, like baking chocolate chip cookies from scratch and concocting meals that would make Emeril rip his apron with jealousy. He was searching for someone who found fulfillment by frequenting the Laundromat, homeschooling the children, and overseeing church potluck dinners.

What he found, instead, was an irresponsible young girl, only two years out of high school, with a determination to leave the small town she grew up in to return to Nashville to pursue a songwriting career, who enjoyed underage drinking and jamming with her guitar-playing friends. Unfortunately for him, he found a girl who lived at home with her mommy and daddy, frivolously spent, never cooked, and thought cleaning meant stuffing dirty clothes under the bed. It's not that he had a problem with women working outside of the home, or even cooking dinner himself. It's just that he was hoping he'd find a woman with a bit more domesticity, someone who would prefer to be at home rather than elsewhere. A woman who wanted to teach Junior about algebra, rather than running out of the house screaming at the very mention of it.

We didn't see eye to eye about everything, and it quickly became apparent that ours would not be the Cleaver residence. Fortunately, Scott was willing to expand his horizons, and I was willing to strive for a bit more domesticity. He didn't have the right to expect me to live for housework, but he did have the right to expect honesty from me, especially when it meant that my past might impact our future.

You always have the right to expect your spouse to be everything he or she vowed to be.

When I was in college, the upperclassmen always told me that boys went to our school for an education, while girls went there to find a husband. Personally, I went there as an excuse to live in Nashville and to find a husband. I did a lot of irresponsible, crazy things while away at school, but I just knew in my heart that if I found the right guy, I would change my ways. And while I couldn't find the motivation to get out of bed and get to class on time, I did find the motivation to date, so I figured I had a pretty good shot of making that a reality. Sure enough, I found a guy and quickly fell not in love, but in lust. But the relationship ended without me having to say "I do," and I didn't have to change one thing about myself. I could go on being stupid for as long as I wanted.

Falling in love with Scott was a shock to me. He wasn't anything like the future husband I had always envisioned. My "dream husband" was at least six feet tall, with a full head of dark hair. Scott is only about an inch taller than I am—which makes him about 5'11". He has blonde hair, which is going gray, and he's balding. My "dream husband" loved books and hiking and was a modern-day man in that he could not only appreciate a new pasta salad recipe, but create one as well. My husband's primary interests are sports and PlayStation. The only books he enjoys reading are video game strategy guides; we've been discussing going on a hiking trip for the past four years, to no avail; and the last time he made dinner from scratch was a steak dinner a few weeks after we were married. I'm telling you all of this with his blessing, only to illustrate the point that Scott was an unlikely candidate to become the love of my life that he is.

Will the Real Julie Please Stand Up?

I now believe that opposites attract, precisely because of my relationship with my husband. He is gentle and kind, and he has a calming spirit. Everyone who meets him automatically feels at home in his presence. When we were dating and engaged, I couldn't figure out what he could possibly see in me. He loved God with every fiber of his being, and I was in the midst of a spiritual crisis, unsure of what, if anything, I believed in. His godly heart drew me, however, and I wanted what he had.

I didn't want him to know just how flawed I was. He was an old-fashioned guy. He wanted a non-drinking, non-smoking virgin. From my perspective, by dating me, he was handling damaged goods. But I loved him, and I wasn't about to risk losing him, so I covered my tracks by manipulating the entire relationship. I wanted to change, but felt so overwhelmed by the prospect of having to deal with the garbage in my life that it was easier just to control which information actually got to him and which information stayed locked up inside of me.

The most challenging balancing act was trying to figure out how much to tell him about the sexual abuse I had endured. To talk about the abuse in general terms meant leaving my husband to guess at the details of what happened. Anyone with some semblance of an imagination can figure most of it out. But there is a true story behind my childhood, and if anyone on this earth deserved to know what was on those pages of my life, it was Scott. Although I knew, intellectually, that what happened to me wasn't my fault, I didn't always feel that in my heart. I hashed everything out with a counselor when I was in high school and believed that I was well beyond feeling shame or guilt, but for reasons I still can't figure out, having to explain it again to the one person I love most in the world brought back feelings I thought had died long ago. So when I spoke of the abuse, I spoke in very general terms.

I once pointed out the man who molested me while Scott and I were out in public, and I almost had to physically force Scott to stay in the car and not leap out to go after the guy.

"I just want him to know that I know," he said.

"Scott, you can't! Please just stay in the car! I never should have pointed him out."

"No, I'm glad you did," he hissed, trying to catch his breath, "because now I can have a little chat with him." He unbuckled his seat belt, and I grabbed his arm.

"Scott ... please don't do this to me! Just let him go!" I was desperate. I envisioned having to call the police to break up the fight.

"I can't just let him go! Nobody hurts my fiancée and gets away with it!"

"But I've forgiven him, and you have to, too." There was a long period of awkward silence as we both tried to find the right words. I knew that he could see through that particular smoke screen—that I was a long way from forgiving him. He dejectedly put the car into drive and pulled away without another word.

Scott may be a tough guy when it comes to protecting the people he cares about, but he has a very innocent worldview otherwise. He doesn't have a laundry list of wrongdoings, and he doesn't know what it's like to stare at the ceiling in bed at night, weighted down with guilt and shame. Just as the number of strange things I did in the past overwhelmed Scott, the number of things he didn't do overwhelmed me. I was not used to dating a guy who said he wanted to lead a godly life and actually pursued it. So I was uneasy about letting him know I was considerably more jaded than he was. For most of my life, I had worked hard at keeping my heartache hidden. I was a master secret keeper, and I was so used to keeping the darkness bottled up inside of me that being transparent was an uncomfortable shock to my system. I hid myself away out of fear and, unfortunately, a desire to manipulate. I could not stand to not be in control.

For example, before we married, he only found out I was a drinker when I took him to a karaoke bar with a few of our friends. In between songs—and I should add that I was still underage at that point—I was ordering Strawberry Daiquiris and Rum and Cokes. And if he thought that night was a once-and-done deal, he got the big picture when he started accompanying me to jam sessions and parties where I drank so much I could barely walk.

I wasn't particularly subtle about telling him that I smoked, either. Scott laughs now at the memory of it. We used to volunteer with a Christian music ministry, working at concert events in the area. Once, after an evening of taking tickets at one such concert, we went to a nearby diner to grab a bite to eat. As Scott was gabbing to me about the events of the day, I reached into my purse, threw a pack of cigarettes and a lighter on the table, interrupted him, and said, "By the way, I smoke." But by the time he found out about the drinking and smoking, he was in love with me. I had "won" him, and I knew he wasn't going anywhere.

I was less than forthcoming about the issue of sex, as well. When we were dating, I simply told him that I had gone too far with an ex-boyfriend my senior year of high school and that I had had a few "bad" relationships. I did not elaborate any further, and Scott, always extremely respectful and protective of my feelings, did not ask.

I was not keeping all of my past information from him, but I might as well have been. I was being very selective about what I shared, and not just about drinking, smoking, and sex. I was tight-lipped about the less significant things that shaped my personality. He knew me as an "out there" personality—at least when I was drunk. I was very shy around people I didn't know, but very engaging around close friends. I had a sharp sense of humor, and when it came to my songwriting, I was mostly confident and determined.

But like a lot of people, much of that was just a facade. I couldn't bear the thought of him finding out that I was always the school nerd—a fat kid who climbed off the bus with gum matted in her hair every day. I didn't want him to know that in high school I was a complete introvert who had three friends and spent lunch periods alone in the bathroom.

While all of these things are rather small issues in the big picture of life, they were huge things to me. I didn't want people to see me as a nerd anymore. I wanted to be respected and, most of all, to fit in. I didn't think either of those things was possible if people knew what kind of kid I had been.

I shared with Scott that depression was an ongoing battle for me, and I even mentioned having attempted suicide as an adolescent. But I made it very clear that it was a resolved issue. He didn't know it, but I was lying right to his face. I still bottomed out and considered taking drastic measures to "remedy" my sadness. My unwillingness to be forthcoming went deeper than just being a distrustful scaredy-cat wife. In reference to the marriage union, Ephesians 5:33 says, "However, each one of you also must love his wife as he loves himself, and the wife must respect her husband." My choice to leave my husband in the dark about some major aspects of my life was a blatant act of disrespect, spurred on by fear. I was afraid that he would want out of the marriage because he couldn't handle my crazy emotions, and I knew if he walked away, I would have even more motivation to attempt something drastic.

It's Not Just About You

When I began writing this chapter, it seemed necessary to get feedback from my "other half," so I sat down with my hubby over a pot of coffee at a local diner and asked him all sorts of questions. I told him I wanted him to be honest—brutally honest, if that's what it took.

"I don't want you to get mad, and I don't want to hurt your feelings," he said quietly. I could tell he was afraid of launching World War III.

"I promise I won't get mad. You have my word on that."

I thought I was doing a pretty good job of hiding bits and pieces of my past from Scott. I honestly believed I was being just subtle enough that I had successfully pulled the wool over his eyes, but as it turned out, I wasn't doing such a fine job after all.

"Every time I asked you questions about something, you changed the subject or told me I didn't need to know about it."

"What do you mean? What kinds of things were you asking me about?"

"Well, anything. You freaked out when I picked up your personal letters or journals. You wouldn't let me read anything. I couldn't figure out why, because I never had a problem letting you look at my stuff. I let you into every part of my life. But with you ... I felt like there was a little closet I couldn't go into, a little *room* I couldn't go into. I felt like you locked a lot away from me."

I was a nineteen-year-old girl, lying across my bed, as Scott sat on the floor reading some of my poetry and song lyrics. (My parents were checking up on us about every five seconds or so.) I had no problem sharing those, and I would often whip out my guitar and play my newly written songs for him. But then I saw him reach for my journal, and I froze. I used to document my entire life in my journal, and the one he held in his hand spanned both high school and my time away at college. It contained the intimate details of just how stupid I'd really been, but, worst of all, it contained my true thoughts—all the ones I vowed I'd never share with another living soul. I reached over the edge of my bed to grab it from him, and he pulled his arm back playfully.

"My, my! Whatcha got in here, hmm? Why are you in such a hurry to get this from me?" He meant no harm. He was just being silly, but I was in a panic.

"Just give it to me, Scott. Don't be a jerk." My voice was shaky, and he picked up on my tone. A sad look spread over his face.

"Why can't I read it? You let me read everything else you write."

"Because it's personal." I lunged at him and swiped the book out of his hand. He got up and walked out of the room, mumbling behind him, "I'm about to marry you. I think that's pretty personal."

I sipped my coffee and watched my husband squirt ketchup on his eggs. The once-distracting chatter of the diner patrons turned into soft background noise. My next question I could have answered on my own, but I wanted to hear it in my husband's words.

"So," I paused, not wanting to finish the question. "How did you feel when you started to realize how much I had been hiding?" There was an even longer pause as Scott leaned on his hand and looked at me.

"Honestly?" he asked.

"Honestly."

"I felt like I had been gypped. Sometimes I thought I could have found someone who didn't have so much baggage to deal with."

Before you take your vows, my advice is to seriously look them over and think about what it will mean to live them out. Get beyond the soap opera fantasy of two wistful lovers dressed to the hilt, whispering flowery words to each other at the church altar. Really dig into what those words mean.

If you can't work up the nerve to tell your spouse when you've officially arrived at the point of "for worse," can you get angry when he or she is not there for you in the midst of it?

When the Tables Are Turned

It doesn't happen nearly as often, but sometimes husbands are abuse victims, and wives are the loving spouses left to fumble in the dark for answers. More commonly, the husbands may have a crazy past, while the wife's childhood sounded like something out of *Little House On The Prairie*.

Take Steve and Jessica. The two met on the Internet, got to-gether in person several times, fell in love, and also married in October 2000. The two came from vastly different backgrounds. Steve's father abandoned his family, and he grew up in a very unstable environment, while Jessica's family has always been intact, and she even grew up in the church. Steve was upfront about some things, like the sexual abuse in his past.

"As we were going for a walk in his old neighborhood, he told me about what one of his neighbors did to him," Jessica explained. "He told me how he was forced into doing things that he did not want to do. He told me how much he hated the people who did that to him for a long time, but he forgave the people now and has a lot of peace about the situation."

But in addition to his own, personal pain, there were other things Steve kept locked up tight, mistakes he had made that he worked very hard to hide. Steve had a number of deep, dark secrets, like his struggles with pornography, tucked way back in the closet, and the revelation of those secrets would later threaten to end their marriage.

"When I found out everything that happened to my husband and what he had done in the past, it built a giant wall between Steve and me. For months I did not want to have anything to do with Steve. When we would go to church or out together, we would act happy. Those who knew us best knew that there was something deeply wrong and painful happening to us. My best friend said that she did not know what to do with me except to pray. I treated her so badly and even yelled at her on one occasion over something petty. I went into a depression and gained at least fifty pounds."

Around this same time, Jessica also discovered the depth of Steve's addiction to pornography and that he had engaged in an inappropriate online relationship, as well.

"I could not trust Steve about anything. Every time he left the house, I had to know where he was going and why. We would argue over what I found on the computer. Since then, we have gotten rid of our computer, and I tote my laptop back and forth to work. I could not trust my husband to be alone to do anything. I felt like a parent. I was on edge at all times. There were times that I wanted to end our marriage and get as far away from Steve as I could. The only thing that I had to hang onto was God. I would not listen to anyone because they could not understand what I was going through. All I wanted to do was sleep, so that I did not have to deal with the problems, or eat myself into oblivion. The refrigerator was my best friend at times."

Jessica went on to explain, "There were times that Steve and I would break into a fight because I thought that he was using the computer. And I bet you he was not even near the computer. It was the trust that was missing in our relationship. The challenge that Steve thought he was facing was restoring my trust, but in the end Steve found something else out: Steve needed to restore his trust in himself. When he was able to come to this revelation, I was sure that the wall was starting to crumble between the two of us."

I understood where Jessica was coming from because I could see myself in Steve. Steve's initial unwillingness to deal with the sin in his life, as well as the sins forced upon him, triggered a sin cycle in his wife. And then, instead of Jessica being the loving, supportive wife he needed, she took on the role of mother and policewoman. Eventually, the anger began evolving into bitterness, taking a toll on every area of their marriage.

"At first, it had a huge impact on our sex life. I did not want to have anything to do with Steve for a long time. I though that not having sex with Steve would punish him. And then when we did have sex, which was not that often, I did not have much of an intimate feeling. I felt distant. But I did want to have sex with Steve because that is what the Bible says we should do. While we were going through the rough times, whenever we had sex, I thought that I was just an object to be used."

A Word to the Spouses of Sexual Abuse Victims

Sadly, it is common for at least one mate to have a history of sexual abuse. So much more in the way of books and study guides is available now than there was years ago, but it's still a "hot potato" topic. No one enjoys discussing it, so they usually don't. Perhaps the most damning part of sexual abuse is the way it makes its victims feel as if there is part of them that is too dirty to be revealed.

Some things are just universal, like the guilt and shame that goes along with having been sexually abused as a child. Probably just about every abuse survivor out there could tell you the same thing—it doesn't go away overnight. And yet, because female sexual abuse is so prevalent and you hear about male sexual abuse substantially less, there are issues that men deal with that we women might not experience as often. It seemed awfully important to at least touch on a few of these issues. Everyone's experience is different, of course, and can be determined by who the perpetrator was, the length of time the abuse occurred, and the age of the victim.

It is commonplace for abuse victims to act out sexually. Some are sexually irresponsible because they are on a quest to feel loved and valued, and some are trying to figure out who they are (many victims are confused about their sexuality, for example), while others use sex to "prove" that they can make another human being happy. Some people—like me—use sex because they buy into the lie that it's all they are good for. Throughout my life, I have had a hard time being able to figure out what my strengths and talents are, much less utilize them. As I grow spiritually and understand what it means to be a child of God, created in His image, I see that I am not here only to be used by others for their own sick pleasure. However, it took a long time for me to see that I am a useful, valuable member of God's kingdom.

But before I grasped any of that, because I felt like such an utter misfit, I wasn't just angry with my abuser, or the abuse itself, but also with God. I saw Him as a big meanie, sitting on a cloud, chucking lightning bolts at me. I figured if God really loved me, He would have stopped the abuse or never let it begin. Just as I shut down with my husband and closed the door to my heart in his face, I did the exact same thing with God.

The Choice Is Yours

A good friend of mine introduced me to the concept that even as God is willing to heal my heart, there is someone else—a formidable foe—who is just as willing to use the cracks in my broken heart to slip inside and work his evil. The thing that I missed for so long, and frequently need to be reminded of, is that choice *is entirely up to me.* Who will I let in?

You could ask yourself the same question. You may not have any seemingly huge problems on the outside, so it may appear that you have it all together. On the inside, however, you have wounds that never healed, and you may be secretly and deeply lost, shameful, and lonely. Your life may not feel like it's crumbling at your feet, but you don't feel like you're truly thriving. You are always a step away from being who you really want to be and where you really want to be.

But, the thing is, you have a choice. You can either accept this as your reality and stay where you are emotionally, or you can open yourself up—and I will admit it requires vulnerability that I am still striving for—to God's ultimate and absolute presence. It may mean acknowledging that, in your woundedness, you did some things you're not proud of. Will you trust God to open the closet door and bring the truth to light, and risk more pain and guilt in exchange for hope and life? Because here is the tricky part: *it may get worse before it gets better.* Living for God does not mean you will have an easy life or a smooth path to travel. Don't expect it. Surrendering your heart to God means you have confessed your willingness to let Him bring your hurt and shame into the light, where it can no longer fester and eat away at your soul.

Think of it like this: imagine you have spent twenty-five years in a dark tunnel that has been, you think, completely blocked off. Your life is one of dank darkness, shame, and fear. You hate the darkness and the chill it puts in your bones, but you're used to it. But all of a sudden, a stream of brilliant light comes blasting through. After so many years in the darkness, that stream of light is intensely painful, burning your eyes, making your head throb, and you hold your arms up to your face to shield yourself in terror. But eventually you start to wonder if maybe, *just maybe*, there exists something better beyond that light—a world of freedom—where you are not bound to one place alone anymore. So you rise to your feet and begin to move toward the light, and the closer you get, the brighter it is, but your eyes adjust, and it doesn't hurt as much anymore. And it is as you had hoped—beyond that light is an exit that leads to freedom and hope. Although it's scary at first, you know freedom is better than fear, and you step out. Eventually, you look back and wonder why you were ever scared of that light in the first place.

It is the same way with a broken marriage. Nothing breaks my heart like hearing about two people who "stay in it for the children," although making that choice will hopefully heal the relationship for real. But I have found that people must "stay in it" because nothing is impossible, and rekindled love and reborn respect is worth hoping for and fighting for! Do you know what those people who stay married for their children are essentially doing? They have decided, for whatever reason, that they have endured too much, the pain is too excruciating, the struggle is too hard, and they have chosen to stay in that dark tunnel until both of them wither away. They are literally living just until they can die.

Nobody wants to sound like a complainer. Most of us would prefer to keep our mouths shut and give the illusion that we have it all together and are handling things just fine. We may even think we're doing everyone (including ourselves) a favor by not being candid. But even if your spouse doesn't know what's going on in your heart, God does. I have gone through much of my life trying to hide something. At times I couldn't even identify the thing I was trying so desperately to cover up. There has always been a part of me that is scared of absolute transparency. Yeah, God knows my inner thoughts and struggles, but it's different when you actually confess them out loud. Silence gives the illusion of safety.

I know there are exceptions to every rule. I know every situation is unique. But I also know that painful doesn't equal hopeless. Maybe you have "hit the wall" in your marriage, and there's nothing more you can do. Even if the reality is that you could do more, but you are in such pain that you don't know what those things are. Give yourself permission to turn the reins over to God. You can't shock or overwhelm Him. Tell Him that you are willing to do anything necessary to save your marriage, even if the process is unpleasant. Remember that "in all things God works for the good of those who love him, who have been called according to his purpose" (Rom. 8:28).

I'm sure you've heard those pesky rumors about women always trying to change their men. I've done that. I've tried to make him more spontaneous in nature, and I've even taken him shopping in an effort to dress him like my own personal Ken doll. (Not that I don't love sweatpants ...) You know how frustrated you feel when you've told your husband two hundred times to watch less television and spend more time talking to you, and he's still glued in front of the tube? Imagine your husband making the effort to reach out to you, to know your innermost thoughts and feelings, and you're working overtime to try to quickly throw a sheet over the skeletons in your closet. Just like it's not fair to try to mold him like a glob of Play-Doh, it's not fair to shut the door in his face when he makes a genuine effort, either.

It may hurt more before it gets better, but we serve a God who is not only sovereign and trustworthy, He is also a life transformer. I have seen the evidence of His goodness in my own life, and it gets easier to trust Him every time I go to Him in prayer. I know He can transform your marriage, too.

Reflections:

1. From what you've read in Matthew 19:6, do you believe that a partner's "baggage" from the past impacts their spouse? Do you think unresolved issues can destroy a marriage? Why or why not?

2. If someone is constantly working to cover up past sins, or forever running from wounds inflicted on them in their youth, how does that affect their relationship with the Lord? And how does their relationship with the Lord affect their marriage?

3. If there are things in your life that you have not con-fronted and/or disclosed to your spouse, what are your reservations?

4. What are some ways in which being upfront and transparent about your past might actually help your marriage?

5. How might your struggles help other struggling couples in the future?

Scriptures:

Matthew 19:6
So they are no longer two, but one.

Psalm 32:3-5
When I kept silent, my bones wasted away through my groaning all day long. For day and night your hand was heavy upon me; my strength was sapped as in the heat of summer. Then I acknowl-edged my sin to you and did not cover up my iniquity. I said, "I will confess my transgressions to the Lord"—and you forgave the guilt of my sin.

2 Peter 2:19
For a man is a slave to whatever has mastered him.

1 Peter 4:8
Above all, love each other deeply, because love covers over a multitude of sins.

Chapter Three

Me, Me, Me ...
It's Not About You

In our bathroom, you will always find either a stack of maga-
zines or a couple of novels. They aren't for decoration, trust me.
For my husband, going to the bathroom is an event, and not
a quick one. Scott has chronic stomach problems. When he's
under stress or pressed for time, God help the fool who gets
between him and the bathroom door.

We have funny stories, but illness has put a major strain on our
marriage at times. My own distance from God made the stress
almost unbearable. I tried to deal with the stress on my own,
but it began to overwhelm me. I began to crumble emotionally
and pushed my husband away. While there was no "magic pill"
to take the stress away, there were some pretty simple things I
could do to be a stronger woman and a better wife—things I
neglected. Recognizing and giving in to those things didn't cure
my husband, but it certainly cured my horrible outlook on life.

It's Not Just Stress or the Wife's Lasagna

I'm not poisoning Scott with my poor cooking skills. His stomach problems are the result of a lovely little genetic blood disease called Hereditary Hemochromatosis. To put it in the simplest terms, he has too much iron in his blood, which is why the disease is also often referred to as Iron Overload Disorder. The iron sticks to everything, including internal organs. Left untreated, it can cause just about every infirmity short of hairballs and hangnails. I joke about it, but the truth is, it can literally rust the body from the inside out and eventually kill its victim. It's definitely not something to be ignored. It can cause cirrhosis of the liver, hormone problems (from iron sticking to the pituitary gland), and heart damage. Some of the other symptoms of Iron Overload include:

- Chronic fatigue

- Redness in the palms of the hands

- Swollen joints and knuckles

- Irritable Bowel Syndrome

- Impotence or loss of libido

Scott has experienced all of the above, and then some. There are many other symptoms, but I've been told I need to keep my word count down to 40,000 ...

To say that Hemochromatosis has had an impact on our marriage is putting it lightly. It nearly derailed us. But this thing is a lot like an untrained German Shepherd that barks and snaps at you. Once you put a leash on the unsightly beast, teach it to sit and shut its mouth, and show it that you are in control, it's not nearly as scary. Scott's chronic illness didn't impact us as much as a basic lack of understanding did. And I, as a wife, jumped into bed, pulled the covers over my head, and refused to face reality for a long time.

I believe that chronic illness is very similar to death, in that there are stages of grief each person must go through before they can fully face the world again. As we painfully found out, it may mean the life you dreamed of together will come packaged very differently than what you imagined. We also discovered that even the most unsightly wrapping could contain precious items of beauty inside.

Too Young to Feel So Dang Old

Scott's a husky guy, with a wide neck and broad shoulders. He has the most muscular legs I've ever seen on a man (*Men's Health* magazine notwithstanding). He could easily be a linebacker. When I met him, he was twenty-seven years old and very fit. Actually, he was pretty ripped. He did manual labor in a factory full-time and worked out. To give you some idea of how strong he was, when my brother and his wife moved out of their condo and into their current home, we were drafted to help. My husband single-handedly lifted and moved their washing machine, while my brother watched in amazement. You could practically see the testosterone wafting through the air. I'm pretty sure men for miles around let out grunts on behalf of their species.

So I wasn't particularly concerned when one night after we had been dating for quite some time, he told me about his illness. I was more concerned about the fact that I couldn't spell it, and I'm a good speller. As I sat there, trying to sound out Hee-mo-kro-ma-TOE-sis, he explained the entire scenario to me because he said it was only fair that his future wife know what she was getting into. I kind of nodded my head and changed the subject. He looked healthy enough, so I just assumed he would always stay healthy. His concern at the time was that I wouldn't want to marry him, knowing there was always a chance he could get sick, but I never seriously considered the possibility.

I had no clue just how serious and merciless his disease would be. And, as I soon found out, it was only the tip of a very large iceberg.

As I mentioned in the first chapter, I was disappointed in our lackluster honeymoon experience, but I wasn't overly freaked out by it. I assumed we were tired and that everything would be fine after we had gotten adjusted to our new life together. But I have to confess ... after I got over the flu and we started having fun on the honeymoon, I was exasperated by the fact there was no sexual activity taking place yet. I tried not to worry—I *didn't* worry—but I was concerned. How could I not be? But after we got into the swing of day-to-day life, I really started to worry. There I was, all of twenty-one years old, in bed with my husband of only a few weeks, and he could not make love. Such a thing is never a fun revelation for anyone, but it's especially mind-boggling when you're still practically a kid and you're still in that honeymoon phase. Tears came easily as I directed a barrage of questions at him. *Do you regret marrying me? Don't I turn you on anymore? Do you think I'm fat? Am I ugly? Are you sure you love me? Is there somebody else?* My sweet, otherwise affectionate husband wrapped his arms around me and did his best to reassure me that it *wasn't* me and there wasn't anybody else. And he was sorry to have to admit he didn't understand it any more than I did.

Reality Bites

After the honeymoon, Scott's health continued to plummet. The most noticeable difference was in his energy level. He was tired all the time and didn't really want to participate in any of our normal activities. Long walks at the park didn't interest him very often anymore. He was seeing a doctor, but I don't believe he had fully accepted that he actually had a *disease* yet. I was the naïve young wife who didn't understand what we were dealing with.

His health wasn't the only thing to plummet, either. His self-esteem began to fade away as our sex life became more and more infrequent, and he was sometimes too exhausted to get off the couch for days at a time. Because his problems seemed to start literally the day we got married, I could not believe that it was out of his control. I thought he must be regretting his decision to marry me, and, instead of actually being fatigued, he was looking for ways to avoid being with me. He told me he was sick and couldn't help it, but I didn't believe him. I saw it as deliberately pulling away from me. It was just too much of a coincidence to me that he "got sick" on our honeymoon. I was frustrated, and every time he told me he didn't feel well, not only did I doubt him, I got angry, too.

One night, I arrived home from work to find my husband doubled over on the sofa. I asked him what was wrong, and he told me he had been having chest pain for several hours. I immediately thought to myself, *"Oh, not again!"* I was tired and frustrated and wanted some peace and quiet. I didn't think I could handle one more crisis, so instead of being a loving, supportive wife, I totally flipped out on poor Scott. I burst into tears and began slamming cupboard doors. "Why can't we just have some peace?" I screamed as I leaned over the kitchen sink, sobbing.

I'm ashamed to relay that story because it breaks my heart to think I could have been so selfish and insensitive toward my husband. My actions told him I thought he was worthless and unlovable because of things he had no control over. And no, we never went to the hospital because Scott sat up straight and said he was feeling better, which he later confessed had been a lie to get me to calm down. I was a world-class jerk.

We are constantly paranoid that he will do himself more harm somehow. Even sneezing brings anxiety. As I write this, my husband knows of three hernias that recently showed up on an ultrasound, and as soon as they start causing him pain, he will need more surgery. There is cautious optimism after each surgery, but also hyper vigilance. They are not major surgeries, obviously. Things could be much worse. He could have much more serious ailments, but that doesn't make the ailments he already has any less painful. Each surgery means missed work and lots of time spent on the couch. I struggle to keep all the balls in the air, and Scott feels guilty that he can't contribute more.

I always wondered if Scott was really sick, too. Every day brought a new complaint, and part of me questioned whether or not he was a bit of a hypochondriac. But after all of his surgeries, I wasn't so disbelieving. He spent literally two years in recovery, off and on. Anyone would be fatigued after that! But by the time I realized it, I had already dangerously wounded my marriage with my insensitivity. As much as I cared for him during the weeks he spent on the couch after each surgery, it could not erase the times I openly accused him of lying or of not wanting to spend time with me. Those were scars always left behind.

The early years of marriage are hard enough under the right conditions, and I might have fared better if I had had some real support. It was mostly my fault that I *didn't* have any because I was stubborn and didn't want to seek it out. Yet people were always asking about Scott, trying to find out if he was doing better or still having the same problems. They rarely asked how I was holding up. They were also quick to put a reassuring hand on my shoulder and tell me they were praying for Scott. Few of them ever said they were praying for me, too. But I needed someone to ask about me and offer up prayers on *my* behalf because I was dying. While Scott tried to get better, all the responsibilities were left up to me. He needed someone strong to turn to, but so did I. I couldn't be there for him the way I should have been, because I never sought out the wisdom of others for *my* spiritual health.

No matter how great a support network you have, living with a partner who is chronically ill will always be hard. Even as I write this book, Scott is suffering from yet another illness that may require surgery down the road. As you can imagine, I'm none too pleased. I don't want to see my husband suffer any more pain. I used to get angry with God for not swooping in like Superman and healing my husband's ailments. It's one of the great mysteries in life, why touching the hem of Jesus' robe could heal some people in Bible times, and some of us today pray consistently for healing and never see it. There are no easy answers, and I can't give you advice on how to sail through life with a sick spouse because it's not possible. (You can't sail through life with a healthy spouse, either!) But just because life isn't easy doesn't mean it can't still be beautiful.

As I write this book, my husband is suffering from Acute Diverticulitis, an illness that may result in surgery to remove part of his colon later in time. He has been sick since before I even started writing, which was several months ago. It has been frustrating to see him in pain, but it has not been nearly as frustrating from a personal standpoint because I was better prepared this time. Taking care of him has made me feel closer to him.

But I didn't just wake up a changed woman. I didn't go from dreading another surgery to feeling honored that God would place this man's care in my hands. I'm learning a lot of lessons along the way.

1. Feelings Follow Actions ... Not the Other Way Around! A good friend introduced me to this concept on a day when my stitched-up husband was virtually immobile on the couch, the house was a wreck, dinner needed to be cooked, and I had to leave for my second-shift job in an hour. Our society preaches that you must first feel something before you can actually do it, and I bought into that lie for a long time. I'm convinced this is how a lot of divorces come to be—people who say they have "fallen out of love" and therefore decide they can no longer go forward in the act of marriage.

Well, I haven't always felt like I was in love with my husband, especially when he couldn't help me with anything around the house for months at a time and the topic of conversation was always doctor bills, the pain he was in, and the amount of drainage from his wounds. In fact, there were times when I felt absolutely numb, but I feel love for him again today because I practiced love even without feeling it. I chose to take my friend's advice and stop feeling sorry for myself and start serving my husband *and* praying for a change of heart. Taking care of him physically and being there for him emotionally actually wiped out the feelings of frustration and resentment and brought back feelings of love. Instead of allowing myself to sink into a depression or go off by myself because of more bad health news, I acted out love. I put him before me and put God's plans above my own.

2. I Surrounded Myself with Believers. At one point in my newlywed life, I became what I call a "Christmas-Easter Christian." It was a rare occasion when I went to church. I was angry with God for what I saw as unwillingness on His part to step in and help us, and I was disappointed in Him for not curing Scott. But I couldn't handle Scott's health issues alone. I was reluctant to tell anyone I needed support. I felt like I should be able to handle it by myself, which was a major pride issue. There was never a really good reason behind it. I'm a firm believer that "church" doesn't have to mean a building with a steeple on it. I suppose it could look like a number of things, but by "church" I'm referring to corporate worship and fellowshipping with other Christians. You can't live in our world as a functioning, healthy Christian without those two things. I know, because I went without those things for a long time, and I was dying spiritually.

So when I finally broke down and sought help among other believers, I did so timidly. I threw it into the conversation that Scott was not well, and could they please pray for me. It wasn't their fault that they didn't ask me how I was doing or if I needed prayer. On the outside, I was "together," so they naturally assumed I was fine. But when I admitted that all was not well, they came to my rescue and prayerfully stood in the gap. They lifted a huge burden off my shoulders and helped me carry it.

Fortunately, not only did my friends pray for me, check up on me, and come to my aid (one friend actually did the dishes in my kitchen sink a number of times), they questioned me about my spiritual life. They would not drop the topic of God. Whether I liked it or not, they pushed me to the cross of Christ. They nourished me on both a human and a spiritual level, and made it possible for me to do the same for Scott.

And yet, I can also tell you I don't do this enough. My natural instinct is to try to cope with everything by myself. Sometimes it takes my friends calling me up and emailing me, saying, "Hey, you need us!" Otherwise, I'd turn my thoughts inward and shut them out despite my need.

3. I Changed My Point of View. One of the results of coming back to God via good friends was realizing that I could see my caretaking as either a burden or a blessing. As I prayed and received counsel, I knew that it was not simply my "job" but a vote of confidence from God. The physical care of my husband was in my hands, and He entrusted it to me. That doesn't mean it was fun, or that I look forward to him getting ill again, but I know that I would not be in this position if God did not believe I was capable of handling it with His help. Furthermore, God has not given me a prison sentence, but an opportunity to fully selflessly serve my spouse.

We may not have an easy life, but we will never go without the equipment we need in order to spiritually rise above our hardships. I figure I must be a pretty "tough cookie" for God to dish out such big responsibilities. When I get sad or overwhelmed, it's the thing I have to draw my mind back to.

4. I Changed the Way I Prayed. Before I was married, I prayed for a long, happy marriage. When our marriage stopped being so happy, I prayed that God would "fix" it. What I was really asking was for Him to make my husband healthy, to give us more money, and to give us the jobs we wanted. We had a little control over our incomes, what we did for a living, and what kind of neighborhood we resided in, but we had no control over health. Knowing this, I prayed even harder that God would heal Scott. Because, after all, if Scott could just be cured, nothing else would seem so bad!

What I learned, painfully, is that despite what we heard growing up, God doesn't always answer our prayers—not when our prayers are outside of His will, anyway. And I came to realize that all the times I begged and pleaded with God to take my husband's illnesses away, maybe I was unknowingly begging God to strip us of a huge ministry opportunity. Living for Christ means being willing to give up everything—even our personal comfort. And that is what my husband and I had committed to do.

From that point on, I still prayed that God would heal Scott. The Bible says, "Let us then approach the throne of grace with confidence, so that we may receive mercy and find grace to help us in our time of need" (Heb. 4:16). I will always hold out hope that God will one day reach into Scott's body and take away his sickness. But my dominant prayer no longer was for Scott, but for myself, that I would become a stronger person, a better wife, and a being more dependent on God because of what my husband was going through. I couldn't fix Scott, but I knew if I sincerely asked God to change my heart and to help me change the way I reacted to hardship, those were prayers He would always answer, no questions asked.

5. I Admitted That I Was Hurting. There is nothing as frustrating as people coming up to you in the early weeks and months of your marriage, asking, "So, how is married life? Are you two having fun?" The expectation is, obviously, that you are having the time of your life—living it up, carefree, no worries. That's why it's called the "honeymoon period." But when you're miserable, worried, and disappointed, nothing hurts as much as having somebody say those things to you. My reaction was always to put on a brave face and tell them that, indeed, life couldn't be any better, and if marriage were any more fun, I'd probably need a sedative. I didn't want to stand there and say, "Actually, Scott is chronically ill, we have no romance in our lives, we're broke, and I think about leaving at least twice a day." But the longer I held it in, and the more I tried to pretend, the harder life became. I had to 'fess up, or I'd fall apart.

I started out only hinting around at my unhappiness. I told a trusted friend, and eventually my mother. Once it became clear that they were trustworthy—that I could tell them how unhappy I was without them judging me as a poor wife or a bad person—the words spilled out, the tears flowed, and the release of it was an incredibly healing experience. The door to counseling, hope, and restoration creaked open the day I "spilled it" and admitted everything was falling apart.

Oh, and by the way … I admitted how I was feeling to Scott, too. I hadn't said anything up until that time, because Scott was sick and I didn't want to make things worse. But, actually, things were getting worse because of my growing silence. When I told him what was on my heart, he breathed a sigh of relief, and we could move forward.

The nicest compliment Scott ever gave me came less than six

months ago, when he wrapped his arms around my waist as I chopped carrots in the kitchen and said, "You're such a different person. You're the best wife in the world, honey, and you're so good to me." I'm not the best wife in the world, but thank God I'm not the worst one anymore! He's right—I have changed. I'm not the overwhelmed, harried person who collapsed in sobs at every piece of bad news. My actions no longer relay the message that I'm depressed from being around such a sick guy all the time. Now my actions let him know that even when times get tough, I'm honored to love and serve him.

And when I have my moments of frustration (I still do), I call one of those friends, or listen to a worship CD, or, more importantly, kneel before God. God isn't ignoring our pain. He has not taken Scott's Hemochromatosis away, and I don't know why, but He has taken our sorrow and replaced it with great joy. He has changed my heart and put countless wonderful people in my path to encourage me. He has given my husband knowledgeable doctors who do their best to make sure he is as comfortable as possible. We are surrounded by blessings—I just had to make myself willing to see them!

But the biggest blessing of all is being able to see past myself and bless my husband in a time of turmoil.

I know firsthand that if you make the effort to bless your mate, God will bless you and your entire relationship in return!

And I also know that my friend's advice was really true—that feelings of love follow the actions of love and not the other way around. When you feel like you can't take it one more day, force yourself to act lovingly toward your spouse.

Reflections:

1. How does suffering cause a person to grow in spiritual maturity? How might it also help a marriage to mature?

2. What does it mean to love another person just as Christ loved the Church? How, then, should we treat our spouse?

3. Based on Ephesians 5:25 and Proverbs 31:10-12, do you think marriage is more about personal happiness or selflessly serving your mate? How might serving your spouse during hard times bring you more satisfaction later on?

4. Why is it important to do loving things for your mate, even when you are tired and frustrated and don't really feel like it? What is the end result of doing that?

5. How might you help a sick spouse to feel valuable and useful around the house, even if they might not be able to physically do very much?

Scriptures:

Romans 5:3
We also rejoice in our sufferings, because we know that suffering produces perseverance.

Romans 8:28
And we know that in all things God works for the good of those who love him, who have been called according to his purpose.

Ephesians 5:25
Husbands, love your wives, just as Christ loved the church.

Proverbs 31:10-12
A wife of noble character who can find? She is worth far more than rubies. Her husband has full confidence in her and lacks nothing of value. She brings him good, not harm, all the days of her life.

Chapter Four

The Icing-Less Cake
(Did I Mention I Really Like Icing?)

I have heard married sex described two ways: it's like the icing on a cake, and it's the glue that holds a couple together. I can relate to the first one, but not the second. Sex makes marriage much sweeter, no doubt about it. (Did I mention that to this day, when I eat a piece of cake, I flip it upside down so I can eat the cake first and savor the icing at the end? That should tell you a little bit about what's coming in this chapter!) It's sweeter, but without the icing, you still have the whole cake. This sex-saturated society tells us that life without sex is hardly worth living, but I'm here to tell you that life, even the married kind, can be worthwhile without S-E-X.

I don't believe that sex is the glue that holds a husband and wife together. In fact, it's one of the worst analogies I've ever heard. Sex is important, but it seems to me like that statement is a huge exaggeration. It's one I've read in books and heard from the pulpit, and I still don't buy it. What is the glue that holds two people together? God. The Bible says that marriage is like a cord of three strands (Eccles. 4:12). When you and your spouse are at wit's end and ready to quit, it's not sex that keeps the cord from coming apart completely—it's God.

That's how I see it.

And that's obviously why I gave this chapter the title I did.

(Did I mention I really, really like icing?)

This is the most emotionally difficult subject for me to talk about. The lack of sex threatened our marriage more than anything else. The shame and humiliation of it splintered our already-weakened relationship. The inability to experience physical oneness with my spouse intensified feelings I had already been trying to push out of my life, like worthlessness and low self-esteem. It also bred new emotions I had not dealt with before. But the same thing that wounded us so deeply as a couple, and so painfully as individuals, taught us about the meaning of intimacy and the rightful place of sex within marriage.

The Loss of Something Precious

Most men dream of marrying a woman with a sex drive that matches theirs, and can't imagine what they'd do with a wife whose drive exceeds theirs. (Besides call all their buddies to brag.) Scott teases me by saying everything makes my temperature rise, even a light breeze.

It's not every day the woman regularly desires sex and the man could live without it, but that has long been the dynamic in our marriage. It didn't immediately start out that way, but it wasn't long after Scott began having trouble functioning that he lost interest in sex entirely. These were not times when he was visibly sick or recovering from surgery. These were times when there seemed to be nothing else wrong.

I did not understand what was happening between us. I knew that Scott had a blood disease, but he had bravely shared the situation with his doctor, who told him he was simply too young to be having those problems—regardless of illness. But his doctor sent him to see a urologist, just in case, for another opinion. And the urologist confirmed what Scott's doctor said; that there was no evidence of physical damage from Hemochromatosis. He suggested marital counseling.

On the afternoon Scott reported the doctor's findings to me, he insisted that he didn't believe it was a psychological issue, but a physical one they hadn't found yet. As much as I love my husband, I am always inclined to believe a medical professional's opinion. All I heard out of that whole conversation was "marital counseling." In my heart, that confirmed the fears I had carried around for so long—that I was fat and unattractive, and the thought of making love to me was revolting to him, but he was too kind to confess it to me. I wondered if he really loved me anymore, in the romantic way a husband loves his wife.

I wanted to go to counseling, but he continued to deny that there was anything psychological behind it, and he didn't want to talk to a stranger about his sexual dysfunction. He awkwardly tried to explain to me how important it is to a man that he be able to "perform." Losing that is like losing a major chunk of his manhood, and Scott was feeling like a failure. I didn't see him as a failure, but I couldn't understand why he would not want to rise above his embarrassment to find a solution to his problem. I believed we could overcome whatever the problem was, be it physical or mental. I just wanted to get some answers and good advice. Scott wanted to wait it out.

So the months passed by, and at first we continued trying to have sex, but our sessions always ended in tears, disappointment, and hurt feelings. It bothered Scott that I could not keep a lid on my heartache, and emotion always spilled out after another failed attempt. I was hurt that he would not seek help and began to feel that he just didn't care. Eventually, the hurt feelings won out, and we gave up trying to have sex entirely. We were not discussing our frustration apart from the periodic emotional outbursts in the bedroom. There was constantly tension in our home, but we avoided addressing it. It wasn't long before all touching stopped, no hugging, kissing, or any of the back rubs we used to lavish on each other. Everything served as a painful reminder that we were living more like brother and sister than husband and wife. I retreated to our office upstairs to play on the computer at night, and Scott stared blankly at the television screen. We even started sleeping in separate rooms.

I felt especially hurt when my friends started having babies. I wondered if I would ever be a mother and under what circumstances. I wanted some semblance of the American Dream. It seemed like nothing else in life would matter if I couldn't have a family. We were too young for our dreams of having a family to be dashed.

When friends came to visit, we pretended to be happy. We were still a cute newlywed couple at church, and we dutifully smiled and shook hands on Sunday mornings, but our visits were becoming infrequent. I didn't dare mention our problems to any of our married friends. Everyone else was "normal," and we were extraordinarily different, and I didn't like it. I desperately wanted at least *that* part of our marriage to be normal. So we pulled away from church and our friends.

Eyeing the Other Side of The Fence

In only two years of marriage, we had managed to completely alienate one another. I was twenty-three and lonely, and I knew I didn't want to live my entire life that way. If I had known there was a medical reason behind our problems, it would have made it much easier to cope, but nobody could point to any cause. And Scott's unwillingness to go for counseling made me believe that he no longer had any romantic feelings for me.

I can't tell you at what point I started "exploring other options," but I had begun making a list of possible scenarios designed to help me escape my miserable marriage. I didn't have much money, and we only had one car. I couldn't throw my belongings in the trunk and disappear in the middle of the night. I had two viable choices: moving back in with my parents, or draining what little we had in our bank account and flying to Nashville to stay at a friend's apartment until I could get my life together. Both seemed drastic and scary, so I ruled them out.

I developed a wandering eye, too. I began to feel like I had gotten married far too early in life and wondered what it would be like to re-enter the dating scene. Old love interests I had kept in touch with on a friendship basis started to hold an allure, and we chatted more frequently. I knew I was playing with fire, but I didn't care. I wanted to feel attractive and loveable again. I was tired of feeling neglected.

Scott would later tell me that he hoped I would do something extreme, so he would have a good reason to leave me. Apparently, a general feeling of unhappiness was not enough for him to do so. In a way, he was deliberately pushing me away in order to push me toward somebody else.

Stirring Up More Dirt

The issue of sex was painful enough, but it was made worse by the fact that I had a very unhealthy view of it because of my abusive childhood. My perspective was a mess! On one hand, I felt unloved and worthless without sex. On the other hand, I felt guilty when it was over. I even felt guilty for having what I now know are normal sexual desires. Rarely were there moments of true joy and intimacy. I was too busy trying to figure out how I was supposed to feel. So when we stopped having sex, everything seemed to intensify, and new problems emerged. Now I was feeling guilty for being upset that my husband and I didn't have a sex life. I felt like I should be able to dismiss it and not be the least bit bothered by it.

All of it seemed so unfair. When I was a child, I had adult sexuality forced upon me, and it altered the way I saw myself, and how I saw the world around me. I was anything but innocent, but I wanted a holy and fulfilling sex life with Scott. Now that I was at a point in my life where I could at least *try* to make that a reality, there was this huge boulder in my way. Sex was no longer something to be ashamed of, and I knew that deep down. I struggled with my attitude towards it because of how I was programmed as a child by sexual abuse, but as a married woman and a Christian, I believed in my heart that sex was *good*. It crushed me that the Lord chose to close that door, for whatever reason.

I didn't know that intimacy meant much more than sex or that the Lord was closing that door in order to lead us through a different one that would breathe new life into our marriage and teach me what intimacy *really* was.

Baby Steps

"Do you want to split up?" I had heard the question swirling around in my mind so many times, but it sounded so brutal coming out of my mouth. Still, it felt good to say it. It was gut-wrenching but necessary. The cards were all out on the table, and we didn't have to tiptoe around each other anymore. But, God, it hurt. Everything seemed to be hinging on his answer, or at least on how I would react to it. If he said yes, would I agree with him, and that would be that? For so long I dreamed of breaking away, but faced with the real possibility of that happening, I wasn't sure what I wanted anymore, and tears ran down my face before he could even speak.

"Do you?" he asked me.

"I don't know. I don't know." I sobbed into my hands. "I mean, I never believed in divorce! I just feel so far away from you, and I'm tired of being so sad all the time!"

There was a lot said in the course of that conversation, and I don't remember most of the specifics. What I do recall is the way my husband pulled off the road and reached out to hold me in his arms, and how being in them felt right, and how the way he softly kissed the tears on my face brought about intense healing in my heart. And I remember that we both agreed we were unhappy, but we still had a little fight left in us, and we wanted to make our marriage not just better but beautiful. Whatever it took, we'd made up our minds that we were willing to do it. By forcing ourselves to discuss our sorrow, we discovered that we still loved each other. Actions led to feelings. And it wasn't the flighty, head-over-heels kind of love that we had known during our courtship. I would liken it more to the will to live. Something had kept us hanging on, even as we considered letting go.

We sat together in the living room long into the wee morning hours, discussing how we were going to save our marriage and make it a thing of joy again. We worked out a battle plan, and the first step was going to church later that same morning and telling our pastor we needed help.

Our meetings with Pastor Doug were difficult at times. We outlined all the things we were having a hard time with, not just the sex, but the sex issue seemed to disturb him the most. He advised us to "start having intercourse." Believe me, if it had been an option, we would have jumped on it without a second thought!

Scott and I knew we had to start touching again, even if there was nothing sexual about it. I shared with him that when he stopped touching me, I took that to mean he couldn't stand to be with me anymore. And when I stopped touching him, he thought I didn't want him to lay a hand on me if there was no guarantee of sexual activity. I stopped touching him because I thought he had stopped touching me, and vice versa. Who knows who stopped first? The point is, none of that was true, but because we also stopped talking, it was a misunderstanding that snowballed.

Once we started touching again, it was like salve on an open wound. It was very deliberate at first. We actually scheduled time to snuggle up in bed or on the sofa. Sometimes it was awkward, but that didn't last long. The same thing we had shied away from felt so natural and perfect. These snuggling sessions usually turned into talking/praying sessions, and we eventually forged a new connection.

We had both made mistakes, but the one mistake we had made jointly—and Pastor Doug helped point this out—was that we stopped seeking God together. We had always struggled with prayer and devotions. There were always distractions keeping us busy, so we always said we'd spend time with God "later." But "later" kept getting pushed back to "never." No one knew about our problems, so no one knew to pray for us. Our cord of three strands was still intact, but we hadn't sought out any spiritual protection, so it was getting battered from every side. We agreed to attend church regularly again and also took the step of calling some good Christian friends. Two weeks later, I stood in front of our congregation and gave a testimony about God's healing work in our lives. It was a step of faith, a way of both thanking God publicly and verbalizing that I had absolute confidence in His ability to bring our marriage up out of the ashes. He responded by sending even more people our way to encourage us.

Rebuilding Trust

During one of our many emotionally charged conversations after we had recommitted ourselves to our marriage, Scott told me very frankly that for our relationship to work, I would have to trust him when he said his sexual problems were mostly physical and not wholly mental. He admitted that even though they didn't start out mental, there was probably a mental element to it now because he knew how much strife it had caused. He was consumed with worry that he would disappoint me.

Regardless of my own insecurities, I had to trust my husband that the root of the issue was grounded in yet undiscovered physical issues. I promised to try, but he in return had to promise to be patient with me.

Eventually, Scott found a new doctor, which meant a lot to me, because I know it was hard for him to trust somebody new with something so sensitive. He did it for us, and I was incredibly proud of him. And this new physician was disturbed to learn that his last doctor had brought the iron in his blood down to anemic levels through frequent Hemochromatosis treatments (phlebotomies), but had done nothing to get those levels back to normal. He also did extensive blood work and discovered my husband had extremely low testosterone, which is a symptom of hypogonadism in Hemochromatosis patients. His last doctor had done similar tests, but never mentioned his testosterone level at all. Scott was forever telling him that his lack of a sex drive and inability to function was ongoing, but his doctor kept sending him away with the promise, "It will get better, just give it time." His new doctor put him on hormone therapy and gave us the hope that it would take a while to work out the correct dosage, but eventually he would get his sex drive back (which it turned out was the main reason he couldn't function—he literally didn't have the physical hormones to!), and it would also give him a lot more energy to get through the day.

I knew how selfish I had been and how insensitively I had handled the situation. Really, I hadn't handled it at all. I had not trusted my husband all the times he pleaded with me to understand that he couldn't help it or that he loved me and still thought I was pretty. He could have said, "I told you so," upon hearing the strangely good news that he had legitimate health issues (as warped as I'm sure that sounds), but he didn't.

For the first time in years, I held out hope that we would once again be able to come together physically. The doctor warned us that due to the nature of Scott's illness, he would probably struggle with dysfunction on and off throughout his life. And through research of our own, we discovered that hormone therapy could cause low sperm count in men, which could impact our ability to have children. But we weren't terribly upset about any of those things because, after all, there's no birth control quite like not having sex! A smaller chance of getting pregnant beats *no* chance. We were also OK with the idea of having sometimes frequent, sometimes infrequent sex, because that was also better than none at all.

Scott had to learn to trust me again after believing for so long that I felt he was useless if he was not able to have sex. He wrestled with the fear that I would leave him if he couldn't perform and we couldn't have children. Simply telling him that I was dedicated to him wasn't enough. I had to go out of my way to show him that I meant business. I had to prove to him that I wasn't going anywhere, and that meant changing the way I interacted with him. I could no longer burst into tears when things didn't go as planned in the bedroom. I could no longer sulk on the couch, mumbling about how I was never going to have children. It was OK to hurt, and it was even OK to show it, but I had to learn the appropriate ways of going about that.

When one of our encounters failed (for lack of a better word), I had to shelf my feelings (because it was no secret what I was going through) and focus on his. I had to grow up, stop crying, and start encouraging. I used to say, "I know it's not your fault, but I'm so tired of this! When are things ever going to change?" I had to stop saying that and instead tell him, "I love you, and no matter what happens down the line, I'm going to be by your side." And when things were especially trying, instead of collapsing in an emotional heap, I had to lift the situation up in prayer rather than tearing it down with negativity. This was not about physical pleasure; this was about emotional maturity. It nearly took losing my beloved husband for me to realize I was one big baby.

Deciphering Truth from Lies

For many years, some Christian attitudes in the Church made sex seem wrong and shameful. Fortunately, as the times changed, so did Christian attitudes regarding physical intimacy, and the topic was suddenly open for discussion. For the most part, I think it's a good thing that we can freely dialogue about such a touchy subject. God created sex, and everything God created is good, so there should be no shame in it.

There is absolutely no shortage of books on how to improve your (married) sex life in Christian bookstores today. Everything is aimed at maximizing a couple's sexual experiences, and it's all under the heading of "reclaiming intimacy." But what about the couples who, for whatever reason, can't have sexual intercourse? Yes, there are ways to be intimate and even sexual without having intercourse, but I think we're doing ourselves a huge disservice by implying that the only way to experience true intimacy is through sex acts. It's simply not true. I would argue that prayer is the deepest, most important form of intimacy there is. I would also argue that since God knows our every heartache and every need, He is more than capable of fulfilling married couples that can't have a sexual relationship.

A relationship can survive without sex, but it can't survive without respect and friendship. In fact, without respect and friendship, the sex isn't exactly much to write home about, is it? Without those two things, sex becomes little more than animal instinct.

It hurts when your husband can't make love to you, but it's *unbearable* when he stops talking to you. Sex really is the icing on a very large cake.

I Saw Behind the Curtain

I'm not as sympathetic as I used to be toward my girlfriends who complain that their husbands want too much sex. I'm not sympathetic at all to the ones who brag about the frequency with which they turn their husbands down. They have no idea the kind of pain it causes. It's like they're stabbing their husbands in the heart, and then laughing about it over a watercress salad with their shopping pals. I know how devastating it is to be turned down, but I was not turned down deliberately. I can only imagine the devastation people go through when night after night their spouse turns them away and causes their frustration to build. I understand the heartbreak of feeling unwanted, and I'm not particularly amused when someone laughs their way through a story about how they withheld sex to prove a point, get revenge, or just be mean.

But I also saw the way harsh criticism affects men. I had always heard that a man's sense of well being and self-esteem was wrapped up in his sexuality, but I thought it was an exaggeration until I saw my own husband torn over the loss of his. All the times I tearfully turned away from him, he knew deep down that he had failed me. The silent criticism was the hardest for him to bear.

Scott exhausted himself apologizing to me, but you might be surprised to find out he didn't apologize for the lack of sex as much as he apologized for everything else he could possibly think of. Usually, however, he made gut-wrenching blanket statements like "I'm sorry I'm not a real man" or "I'm sorry I'm not everything you need." If he had been 100 percent flawless otherwise, he still would have felt like a failure. It was that important to him. Long after we recommitted ourselves to our marriage and Scott became a wonderfully affectionate, loving, prayerful partner, he would still grow very quiet at times. After I pleaded for him to tell me what was wrong, he would again apologize for not meeting my supposed expectations.

So much of who your husband is lies in his sexuality, and when you constantly refuse his advances, you might as well be refusing all of him. God gave you the gift of sex to bring you together. Don't use it as leverage against each other. Determine in your heart to make it a blessing and not a weapon.

Here and Now

God has not fully restored this part of our life together. Sometimes things happen, sometimes they don't. We rejoice when we are able to be physically intimate. I won't tell you it's easy, because it's not. I have to give my fear of not being able to have a family to God all the time because it creeps up on me at the most unexpected times.

I have hope that we'll eventually have a regular sex life, but I've also come to a place where I know I can accept it if we never do. We have a happy, intimate marriage. If I had my way, regular sex would be a part of it, there's no denying that. But if everything else in our relationship is solid, then going without sex is survivable. I don't doubt my husband loves me, and he doesn't doubt my devotion anymore.

Going without sex has helped me to see the differences (and the similarities) between sex and love and gain a healthier perspective. God has used this to reverse some of the crazy ideas that were planted in my head by sexual abuse, like believing it was all I was good for and that the only way to make someone happy was to give in to sex.

When Scott and I do touch, when we are able to be physically intimate, it's new and exciting, like we're newlyweds. It's a fresh start all over again, and we savor our time together. God has brought good out of our pain.

Reflections:

1. Why is regular sexual activity with your mate so important?

2. What is your idea of intimacy? Do you think it's possible to achieve physical intimacy without intercourse? Do you think you can be sexual without actually having intercourse?

3. If you have a "normal" sex life with your spouse, have you ever considered how you would handle the loss of that physical relationship? Have you ever discussed it together? What sorts of things would you do to continue on in a happy marriage?

4. If God is the strongest strand in the "cord of three," then a couple can know that when their own strength is gone, God can hold them together. Knowing this, which do you think is more intimate: prayer or sex? Can one enrich a couple without the other? Why or why not?

5. Why do you think so many couples have a hard time communicating about sex?

Scriptures:

1 Corinthians 7:3-4

The husband should fulfill his marital duty to his wife, and likewise the wife to her husband. The wife's body does not belong to her alone but also to her husband. In the same way, the husband's body does to belong to him alone but also to his wife.

Ephesians 4:2

Be completely humble and gentle; be patient, bearing with one another in love.

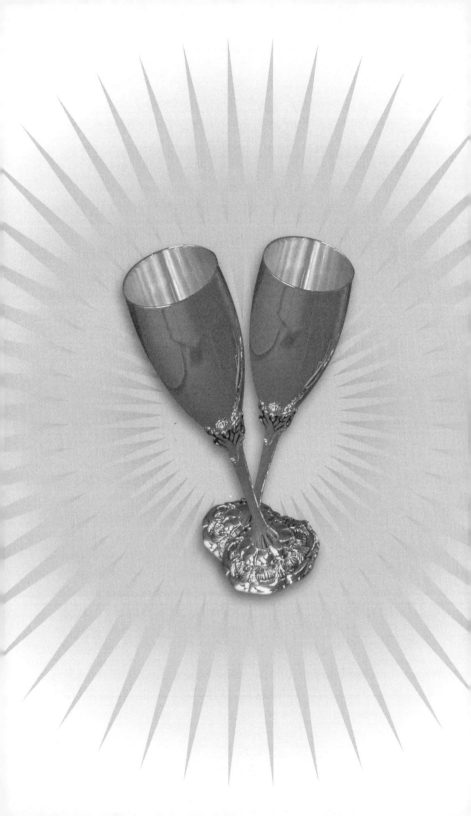

Chapter Five

Losing Your
Financial Footing

Marriage is supposedly economical. Two incomes are better than one, after all. When I was single, I lived at home with my parents, worked full-time, and had no expenses to speak of. I never had a shortage of cash, and I was the cool friend who always took everybody out to dinner. When Scott asked me to marry him, it did cross my mind that perhaps I should start putting some money into savings, but I figured if I had money when I was single, I'd be rolling in it once I got married.

But unexpected expenses popped up, and poor planning made our bank account seem more like a minefield than a bountiful harvest. While sex was our biggest heartache, money was our biggest stressor. It was the one issue we weren't silent about in our marriage ... mostly because we were constantly screaming at each other over it. We argued about which bills were more of a priority and who should control the dough. We also hid from the landlord together. It turned out we were not alone in our landlord dodging or in eating some variation of macaroni and cheese three nights a week.

A few months ago, I was asked to write an article about pre-marital counseling, so I posted a survey online asking people about their counseling experiences before they were married, and its relevance in their lives once they tied the knot. In my survey, I asked couples what issues they struggled with the most after they got married. I got several hundred responses, and overwhelmingly people told me, "Finances!" Maybe we all need somebody to take us by the hand and show us how to budget our money after all.

Since we're still trying to find our way out of debt (you can't build Rome in a day), maybe I'd better stick to giving you some insight into how not to get into debt in the first place!

Starting Out Stupid

When we were dating, Scott and I liked to live it up. Our dumbest premarital mistake (second only to having sex) was that we threw away dollar bills like they were miraculously re-generating in our wallets. We had a lot of fun and went on some pretty elaborate dates, but we never started a nest egg because we were two naïve, bleary-eyed lovers who never thought we'd need some extra bucks to fall back on. We really thought we'd always have more than enough. I grew up with plenty of money, so I never knew what it was like to go without. I couldn't even comprehend it. My husband, on the other hand, grew up poor, so he loved the fact that as an adult he could afford pretty much anything he wanted, and he certainly bought anything he wanted.

As I said, we didn't save any money while we were dating, and that didn't change after we got married. Saying "I do" didn't suddenly instill a sense of financial responsibility in either of us. But the big crash didn't happen overnight. We didn't go out and buy a mansion we couldn't afford or anything like that. We were upstanding citizens at first. We both had good jobs, which meant we made good money, which meant all the bills were paid on time. When we were first married, we even paid some of our bills early. There was always plenty left over for fun ... though strangely enough, not for a savings account. Funny how that happens!

I entered into our union driving a 1992 Geo Metro. You know, the little blue things that sound like they have a rubber-band propeller under the hood instead of an engine. It was about as safe as a cardboard box on wheels, but I could fill the tank on $10 and make it last for a week. I bought it from my brother very cheaply.

After Scott flipped his 1995 Hyundai Accent into a tree a few months before the wedding, we decided we wanted something new, so we went car shopping, and instead of wisely choosing a nice-but-cheap used car, we bought a brand new one ... on my soon-to-be husband's poor credit. It wasn't exactly an expensive luxury vehicle, but we were paying $340 a month on it. The thing cost twice as much to fill up and guzzled gas. So even though it was nice, we began to hate it with a passion.

We were also introduced to quite possibly *the* most dangerous material made of plastic on this earth—credit cards. Since we both worked for a large bank at the time, credit was easy to come by. We had purchased some furniture on my card prior to the wedding, and after we got married, we used it to partially fund our extravagant first Christmas, buy new clothes, and purchase anything else that caught our eyes. It wasn't long before it was maxed out, but we weren't worried! In the beginning, we were more than able to make substantial, sometimes double payments.

Ah, but we also needed a new computer. The one I had been

using for the last six years was on its last legs, and it was time to purchase one that didn't shut down every five minutes. We marched ourselves over to the computer store the first week we were married, where I applied for and received more credit. Our $1,800 computer was delivered a week later, and as usual, we weren't worried about our payments because there was a steady flow of income to our bank account.

All the while, we lived from paycheck to paycheck. Money was in abundance on payday, but by the end of the week, we were nearly broke because we did nothing but spend, and what cash wouldn't cover, we bought on credit. As long as we paid our rent on time, kept up with our astronomical car payments, and had some left over for dinner and a movie, we felt like we were "successful."

The first months of our marriage were like the calm before a storm. Everything was so perfect—we had no idea what was around the corner.

Well, I Didn't Expect THAT to Happen!

"All good things must come to an end." Cliché but true, yet we totally ignored the warning. We thought if things had started out so great, they could only get better. When I was engaged and running around showing everyone my new diamond, I confessed to a few friends and coworkers that I was a little worried about having to leave home and take care of myself. I wasn't sure how to do that, and since Scott had never lived alone, I wasn't sure he knew how to do it, either.

But once I signed my John Hancock on the line of a credit slip for the first time, I was empowered enough to honestly believe that we would always have plenty and never be in want. I was guided by immaturity and fueled by the allure of new stuff. And to be honest, I was a little high on myself. I thought, *Wow, I'm twenty-one years old, I'm married to a great guy, and we have a three-bedroom house on Main Street in a quaint little town, two cars, and white-collar jobs.* I felt like I had "arrived." Sure, our relationship was suffering because of secrets kept and a lack of communication, but heck … we had THINGS!

So imagine my horror when, six months into married life, I lost my well-paying bank job. Actually, the money part wasn't the horrific part at first. The other employees had become like a second family to me, and I actually mourned the loss of being with them. Not that we couldn't call each other up on the phone, but they had become my sounding board for my marital discord, and it sort of felt like my therapist just up and died. To recover, I informed my husband that I would be "taking a week off" and begin my job search after my little mini-vacation.

But a job was hard to come by. I had many interviews, but they never seemed to pan out. It took four months before I found another job, and since we had no savings, the bills fell behind. Everyone was sympathetic toward us at first, but after a month or two, they started to lose patience. I had to resort to the ultimate low among married people—hitting up my parents for money. They were very kind to us. They understood hardship and lovingly wrote checks in our name. But even my father started to say, "You're killing me, kid."

My new job was unlike any job I'd ever had before. I was hired to work full-time in a group home for six adult males who had developmental disabilities. It was scary at first because some of them had challenging behaviors, and I had to bathe and dress them. But I came to really love my job, and I made new friends, so it didn't take long to adjust. It was especially nice to have a second income since our landlord was threatening to evict us by that point.

About a month after starting my new job, my car was side-swiped on the driver's side by a minivan. I don't remember much about the accident itself, only fragmented images of having to climb to the other side of the car to get out because my door was so smashed in and of "waking up" in the grass alongside a cemetery. The accident left me with a severed tendon in my left hand that required surgery, thirteen stitches in my left knee, a concussion, glass in my mouth, and more cuts and bruises than I could count. And being a new employee meant no short-term disability coverage. I was out of work for more than a month recovering from my injuries, so we never even had a chance to catch our breath or pay off any old overdue bills.

That little job loss was the start of problems that would span the course of years to come. Only a few months after my accident, Scott lost his job and was out of work for a long time. He also started having his many surgeries, which required me to take off work to care for him, and I lost my job teaching occupational skills to adults with disabilities after that.

How poor were we? Poor. So poor that we had to lean on both our church and our parents for quite some time to keep us going. At some point, guilt and humiliation overwhelmed us, and we couldn't ask for help any more. We decided the only way to get back on our feet again was to move out of our big house and downsize to a cheap apartment. We had picked our first apartment based on the notion that we were going to have kids a year after we got married. It was sad packing our things, knowing that we weren't anywhere near being able to start a family, both for financial *and* physical reasons. But the move was necessary, and we knew it was what we had to do to secure a better future for ourselves. Besides, our landlord was beyond thrilled to see us go. It was definitely time to move on.

Taking that step was one of the best decisions we ever made. Our apartment was a lot smaller, but it was also a lot homier and close to $100 cheaper! After the move, Scott picked up part-time sales work, and I started doing freelance advertising copy for a local newspaper on the side. The extra income allowed us to live within our means for the first time since we walked down the aisle.

The Positives and Negatives of Being Broke

I was the first one in my group of friends to get married, and I was very young. But I was pretty proud of how I started out married life. We had a nice house full of new furniture, two cars, and great jobs. It wasn't until my friends started getting married and buying new houses and new cars and having babies that I started to feel left in the dust. They were moving forward in their careers, and I was a struggling freelance writer desperately searching for a day job. My friends built white picket fences while I pulled the shades and waited for the landlord to stop pounding on the door and go away.

People like to romanticize being young and poor, and I don't know why. There is nothing romantic about it. When you don't have any money and you can't pay your bills, people start viewing you as a lowlife, and the only way to survive is to become one. You avoid people and situations because you know you owe money. It gives a very poor Christian witness, and it haunts you for a long time. It's easy to fall into financial despair, but it takes forever to get out of it. (We're still digging out of our hole.)

Our first Christmas together had been nothing but a giant spending spree, but the years following definitely were not. I started to dread what was once my favorite time of year because I knew I could either buy people semi-decent Christmas presents or eat. I wanted to shower my niece and nephews

with gifts, but I couldn't. My mother would call me just after Thanksgiving and say, "Don't spend money on any of us.
Nobody expects you to." Her words were meant to comfort
me, but the fact that "nobody expected me" to buy them good
presents was a knock to my ego, and it was even worse for my
husband, who was already feeling like a failure as a provider.

But being broke knocked me off my pedestal, and maybe that's
what I needed. Maybe that was God's intention all along in
allowing this to happen. Maybe I was a little too cocky and in-
dependent, and what He most wanted was for me to realize that
without Him everything is worthless and destined to fail. Not
having a dime to my name forced me to turn to God, and this
time it was hard to be angry with Him because He pulled off so
many miraculous stunts.

To my astonishment, on more than one occasion I received
a random check in the mail for the exact sum of money I
needed to pay one bill or another. Or I'd go to make a pay-
ment, and it was already listed as "paid" in their computer
system. It was impossible to miss God's hand in the midst of
our struggles. I was often confused because God's presence was
so obvious in our financial situation, yet it was so hard to find
Him in our other troubles. I could not understand that at the
time, but I now see that, for whatever reason, He was using that
part of our marriage to show us that He was with us and that
we could trust Him in everything else, as well. I don't know
why He revealed Himself in that way and not in others, but I
do know I was foolish not to have picked up on that message
loud and clear. If God could find a way to get our electric bill
paid when we had no money whatsoever, He could certainly
help us restore intimacy in our marriage.

Being broke also made us put some serious thought into what
we wanted out of life. Scott had left the field of banking to

work with troubled kids, which was where his heart was, but it didn't pay nearly as well. However, the fact that his job would pay for him to go back to school seemed worth the cut in salary, so he decided to stay. I started working with teenage mothers, but my focus continued to be on writing. I wanted to get paid for my work and to eventually make it my career. Since we were already penniless, it seemed there was no better time than the present to chase that dream, so I threw all my energy into freelancing.

We also learned resourcefulness. Remember all the times your mother scolded you for leaving the door open in the winter, asking, "Do you think I'm trying to heat the whole neighborhood here, or what?" Mom's nagging makes a lot more sense when your lights are on only by the grace of God and the tolerance of a nice electric company worker. And I, the woman who leaves the TV on when nobody is watching, had to realize that even the night-light in the hallway costs money to run.

I had to learn another lesson my husband had been trying to teach me from day one—that most generic food tastes exactly like its name brand counterpart. It seemed kind of goofy worrying about a $0.13 variation in types of pasta, but when you calculate all those subtle differences, they begin to add up.

Our budget meals consisted of a lot of spaghetti and macaroni and cheese. Macaroni and cheese with tuna and peas mixed in it became the meal of choice in our home. We heard about mixing Spam with macaroni and cheese, but we weren't brave enough to try it. Of course, when we had a craving for some "real" meat, we cut up hotdogs and threw them in the pot. We tried just about everything short of dumping Lucky Charms in. (It probably would have tasted better than Spam!)

Don't Worry ... Everybody Else Is Broke, Too

I mentioned at the beginning of this chapter that when I posted a random survey on the Internet, the number one struggle among young couples, far and wide, was money. I asked couples the question, "What are the issues *you personally* struggle with in your marriage?" Here are just a few of the answers I received:

Finances, prioritizing the marriage. So many other things seem to come first, even insignificant things.

Trying not to argue about money issues.

Money management. I try to manage the money, and my wife tries to spend it.

Money is an issue.

We are getting control over the money issue but past mistakes take some time to conquer.

Did I say finances??? I'm starting to think that there may be something under "finances." I'm just not sure what.

I think we have struggled at bit with the money aspect. We make a fine living, but we have different views on how to spend (what we earn).

I know very few people who entered married life with their dream career, a beautiful home, and more money in the bank than they knew what to do with. Those people are few and far between, and if you compare yourself to them, you'll never measure up. Most of us aren't high-powered doctors and lawyers, and even those people spent eons of time in school, for which they will be paying off loans until they retire. When we

lower your own credit score. I should have stopped applying for credit and saved those points for the many, many employers who would be checking my credit after I lost my jobs. (Which, by the way, is another reason to have as good a score as humanly possible!)

Grocery Shopping

If you go shopping once a week and buy everything you need at once, you will save money. Make a list and cut your coupons. It makes a real difference! When I know exactly what I'm going to buy, on exactly what day I'm going to buy it, that closes the door to other "petty purchases" ... to use one of my mother's favorite phrases.

My husband and I love to eat, which is what makes frequent shopping trips such a dangerous thing for us. We're more likely to grab an extra bag of chips or throw another six-pack of soda in the cart "just in case we run out." And since we're frequent Wal-Mart shoppers, I'm just as likely to grab a new eyeliner as Scott is to grab an unneeded video game. It's just human nature that if you see something you want, you'll make up an excuse to buy it. Save yourself the hassle by setting aside an afternoon and creating a shopping list.

Give Yourself an Allowance

Do you like stuff? I love stuff. If you were to unleash me in Barnes & Noble with $1,000, I'd come out a few hours later a very satisfied woman. The same goes for record stores and any store that sells clothes, shoes, and body lotion. In my single days, I used to stop at the ATM and take out $400 to blow at the mall, and I wouldn't think twice about it. But that stopped when I got married, and suddenly I had to pay rent, utilities, car repairs, credit payments, etc.

When my husband and I get paid now, we set aside enough to go on a date, and we each take $20 as "play money." That way, if I want to buy a new book or something, it's already built into the budget. We're not tapping into nonexistent funds.

Stop Comparing Yourself to Other People

A woman who has been a good friend of mine since the sixth grade seems to have everything. She was one of my bridesmaids. She got married less than a year after we did and promptly bought a house and two new vehicles. Shortly thereafter, she gave birth to twins. And shortly after that, her grandmother passed away and left her and her family a large house, which meant they could pocket all of the money from whichever house they chose to sell. For a long time, I looked at her life and thought, "Why isn't that me?"

Well, it doesn't really matter. I'd love all of those things, but I don't have them. I am learning contentment. It has not come easy. I want my brother's stone house and beautiful gardens. I want my friend's SUV. I'd love to sell my 1994 Pontiac—the one that bucks over 40 mph—and buy something new and shiny, with a Hemi under the hood. I'd love to live somewhere I can't hear my neighbor's private intimate moments through the ceiling. But I live where I live, and I drive what I drive. I can either be content with my present situation and work toward a better future, or I can get stuck in the mire of wanting what everybody else has right now. I'm learning jealousy only makes you bitter, but hard work reaps rewards.

Suck It Up and Ask for Help

You have a few choices here, and they're pretty cut-and-dry. Either you go it alone and miss more payments and throw more dirt on your own grave, or you swallow your pride and ask for assistance. I'll be blunt here—asking for help totally sucks.

There is nothing quite as humbling as having to ask somebody for money, especially when you know your own irresponsibility played a big role in your empty billfold. But the Bible says that if we don't have something, it's because we haven't asked God for it (James 4:2), so if you're shivering in the dark because your electricity was shut off in the middle of February due to issues of pride ... well, that's your own fault, too. Depending on how humiliated you're feeling, shivering in the dark may seem like the better option, but I'd imagine that would get old pretty fast.

One important thing I'd like to add to this section is a reminder that the people sitting next to you in church are your relatives in Christ. Their purpose is not to sit there and look nice and proper. Brothers and sisters in Christ are there to love and serve one another. If you are genuinely in need, there is nothing shameful about telling your church family about your situation. It's biblical, and God has called us to respond to the needs of others. I'll admit, although we were told the exact same thing, it was still hard to put our pride on the shelf and ask for assistance, but our church family blessed us in a big, big way. We were truly shown God's love, and that love helped to quiet our fears.

Before I lost my first job, I never understood why a married couple would get divorced over money. It really seemed rather petty to me, but that was before I was constantly bickering with Scott over every little dime. Money is stressful when you don't know how to manage it. The *best* advice I can give you is to make sure you stick together along the rocky road. No one enjoys being financially stretched. Remember that you're in this together, and if you're feeling stress, chances are your partner is, too.

Most of all, be patient with yourselves. This is *not* the end of the world. (It just feels like it!) It's so easy to fall into financial trouble and so hard to climb out of it. It won't happen overnight. In fact, it might take years. But you will learn from it if you allow yourselves to be teachable. Let humility win out over humiliation and pride.

I promise you there is a world beyond macaroni and cheese and Dollar General Christmas presents.

The question is: even if there was nothing beyond all of that ... would you be content enough to make your marriage work?

Reflections:

1. Think about your family's financial status when you were a child, and your financial status before you were married. How did this impact your expectations of what married life would be like?

2. Have you been pleased or disappointed with your finances since you've been married? Why?

3. What does the Bible say about financial responsibility? Why might the Lord allow a couple to go through a long stretch of being "in want"? What lessons could be learned from going through that, as it relates both to marriage and our relationship with God?

4. Why is it so important to God that He can trust us with money? If we are not trustworthy with worldly things, what does that say about us spiritually?

Scriptures:

Proverbs 3:25-26

Have no fear of sudden disaster or of the ruin that overtakes the wicked, for the Lord will be your confidence and will keep your foot from being snared.

Philippians 4:12

I know what it is to be in need, and I know what it is to have plenty. I have learned the secret of being content in any and every situation, whether well fed or hungry, whether living in plenty or in want.

Luke 16:10-12

Whoever can be trusted with very little can also be trusted with much, and whoever is dishonest with very little will also be dishonest with much. So if you have not been trustworthy in handling worldly wealth, who will trust you with true riches? And if you have not been trustworthy with someone else's property, who will give you property of your own?

Chapter Six

I Love You,
No ... I Hate You

I remember the day I was diagnosed with Bipolar Disorder because I could not believe I had it. Even though it runs in my family, I thought there was another explanation for my ups and downs and overall weirdness. There were more bad days than good ones, and sometimes even my good days weren't all that good. I had very few "happy" days, and that's why I didn't believe I was bipolar. After all, the outdated term for BP is "Manic Depression," and I didn't feel manic. I thought that in order to be a "manic depressive," you had to go around in a state of euphoria. My life resembled an episode of Dr. Phil, not a screen shot from *The Sound of Music*.

I knew I was making my husband's life a living hell, and I was in a constant state of confusion and frustration. It took a lot of patience for my husband to live in the same house with me, and it took a lot of patience for me to make him understand how to respond to me.

Everybody gets depressed, and when you look at the numbers, it seems like everyone on earth has some form of mental illness. Sometimes healing from mental anguish can be found in a romantic weekend away, a couple of days off work, or a few counseling sessions. But my mental health issues were rooted much deeper, and all the quick fixes I tried seemed to make things worse. Because I didn't understand the full scale of what I was dealing with, my husband was at an even greater loss because of my erratic moods and behavior. It was hard for him to live with someone who was a doting wife one minute and a plate-throwing lunatic the next. A lack of understanding on both our parts almost made him walk out the front door (as plates and silverware crashed against the walls in the background!).

Understanding the Nature of the Beast

Everybody has gone through periods of sleeplessness. Sometimes it can be attributed to stress or to drinking too much coffee. Other times, you just can't get comfortable, so you're up punching your lumpy pillow at three o'clock in the morning. You toss and turn in bed for a few nights, and you feel like a truck has hit you when you go to work.

Well, I experience sleeplessness all the time. It usually lasts a few weeks, not just a couple of days. When I am lucky enough to drift off, I wake up two, three, even four times a night and struggle to get back to sleep. Sometimes I wake up once and that's it—I'm not going back to sleep at all. I remember the nights I sleep well because they're rare.

I don't feel exhausted when I can't sleep, though. I'm wide-awake and full of energy. When I'm in bed trying to sleep, my mind races, and I jump from one thought to the next. Sometimes my brain moves at such warp speed, my thoughts don't make sense anymore. The longer I try to force myself to sleep, the worse it gets, so I get up and try to write, or get online (which is one of the worst things I could do because it's interactive and makes me more awake). I've even been known to wash dishes and straighten up the house in the middle of the night. It's frustrating not being able to sleep because I know eventually I will experience "the crash."

During these sleepless, energetic periods, I'm very creative and motivated. I take on tasks I couldn't possibly handle realistically. I talk a lot and can't shut up. Mania is an annoyance, and it is frustrating not being able to sleep or slow my thoughts down, but at least I get things accomplished! It is a period of great creativity. I spend most of my time jotting down new writing ideas. I return to songwriting, however briefly, and feel like I have something to offer the world.

Depression is what robs my joy. It's not just a feeling of being sad or wanting to take a day off work to sleep; it's this sense that all of life is absolutely bleak and hopeless and nothing you do will ever change that. My sense of reality and my ability to reason virtually disappear. On a "typical" bad day, I know that tomorrow is a new beginning, and I believe that God allows everything to work together to fulfill some grand plan of His. But when I'm clinically depressed, there are no tomorrows. And worse yet, I don't care. Instead of feeling that I have something to offer the world, I start believing the world would be better off without me. I am hyper-aware of all my flaws, big and small, past and present.[1] There have been times when the only thing holding me back from suicide was a deep fear of hell and my theological confusion in that area. Note that I didn't say my hope in Christ held me back. No, it was fear that held me back.

For a long time, my depression absolutely alienated my husband because I retreated and wouldn't discuss it with him. I told other friends when I was feeling desperate, but I didn't tell him because I didn't want him hovering around me. I mostly wanted to be left alone. I didn't think I could stand to hear him constantly asking, "Are you OK? How are you feeling today?" So I shut the door in his face, crawled under the blankets, and disappeared.

When I was fifteen, I had earned a reputation for being a mental case at school. My parents were about ready to send me away or divorce me or whatever was the quickest, least-painful thing to do. I went to see a psychiatrist. She was about 6'1" with platinum blonde hair, huge Sally Jesse Raphael glasses, and diamonds on her hands that probably weighed about as much as a small ham. She peered at me over her glasses while I rambled aimlessly, occasionally scribbling something down in her notebook. She intimidated me, but she recognized clinical depression and wrote out a prescription for a little blue antidepressant pill. I didn't put much thought into whether it was right or wrong, whether it would control my personality or not. I was miserable enough that if she had told me to drink from my toilet twice a day for guaranteed relief, I would have done it.

And the way I see it, those little blue pills saved my life. A few weeks after I started taking them, I noticed that I was able to handle stress better. I wasn't running through the streets shouting with joy, nor was my personality altered, but I wasn't constantly trying to find a reason to live, either. For the first time in my life, I felt almost "normal." I found some peace, and I even noticed that my on-again, off-again relationship with God seemed to be more even keel. I still suffered through bouts of depression, but they didn't last as long and were less severe. I also expanded my sexual abuse counseling from just my support group to individual therapy as well.

I ended therapy during my senior year of high school and went off the antidepressants soon after. I did OK without them for a while, but the older I got, the more I could see the depression creeping back into my life. By the time I reached adulthood, my depressions were just as frequent and severe as they had been in my youth.

Married Life, Scary Life

One of my most amazing feats in life was convincing my husband that I was a normal person. He knew about my past when we were dating—the depression, the suicide attempts in high school, the abuse, all of that. But he was under the impression that after many years of counseling and taking antidepressants, I was healthy again. He didn't know that just weeks before we met, I had been suicidal again.

At first, there was no intended cover-up going on. Falling in love with Scott brought a lot of joy and excitement to my world, as well as new friends and situations. Everything seemed fresh and wonderful, and I was genuinely happy. I had down times, but I loved being with Scott and I was looking forward to our life together. I built my world around him, and I was in a love-induced haze right up until we got married.

But after the wedding, that pesky little thing called reality kicked in. As the newness wore off, the old familiar feelings of emptiness came back in full force, and they were so strong I couldn't hide them anymore. My husband had no idea that his sweet, loving bride could turn on a dime and morph into a raging psychopath.

The first time he encountered The Wrath of Julie was just a few months after we were married. We had invited another couple over for dinner. I had worked my fingers to the bone cleaning the house, and I'd done all the grocery shopping for the elaborate (and probably too difficult) meal I had planned. But there was a snowstorm forecast to hit that night, and our friends, who lived about an hour away, called to say they weren't coming because they didn't want to take the chance of getting stuck in bad weather.

I had been up for a week straight unable to sleep. Planning a huge meal and making the house look spotless gave me something to do as my thoughts raced at warp speed and my body fought to find rest. But when I found out our friends weren't coming, I lost it. It was mild disappointment (because it really wasn't a big deal) and severe exhaustion combined, and the weight of it made me snap. Poor Scott. I'll never forget the look on his face as I knocked over one of our dining room chairs and said things that would make a bartender blush. But that's just where the rampage began. For the next several minutes, I yelled and cursed, throwing things, hitting things, kicking things, all while my husband stood in the exact same spot with his mouth hanging open, speechless. As Scott looked around the kitchen in horror, my rage turned into shame, and I ran to our bedroom, crying hysterically.

I tried to explain to him that I couldn't help it, or that it certainly felt that way. It felt like a huge surge of anger. I could tell when it was coming, but I didn't know how to stop it. I didn't want to react like that. I knew it was wrong, and it always zapped me of so much energy, but I felt powerless over it. It had always had a grip on me, and I actually felt even less in control of my temper when I was younger. I told my husband these things, but I know if the tables had been turned, I probably would have thought he was a nutcase. I was the equivalent of an

F1 tornado. I only left a minor path of destruction in my wake, but I was still a frightening force to be reckoned with.

I further exacerbated my husband's confusion by flip-flopping between enraged and seductive. Need I remind you my husband has suffered some pretty serious health problems for a long time now, and sex hasn't exactly been a priority? So even if I'd spent the day cleaning the house, making myself look perfect, and had given him a two-hour massage, physiologically—by no fault of his own—he would be relaxed and happy, but not desiring sex. But do you know what totally turns a guy off? Flipping out on him. Imagine that!

Sex was a cycle in itself. I was irritable, but I also wanted sex. In fact, it became my primary focus. It didn't matter how much work was piled up on my desk or how many dishes were dirty in the sink, all I could think about was how to get sex. I knew I couldn't get it from Scott, but I tried anyway. When it didn't happen, I felt angry and hurt and rejected. That, of course, made me want to fling more stuff across the room. But who could blame the guy, even if he was rejecting me? I hadn't exactly created a sensual environment, overturning chairs and such.

Learning the Ropes

As you may recall from the first chapter, my husband grew up in a family that never yelled. I didn't believe him at first, because in my family you weren't having a conversation unless you were trying to one-up the other person in decibels. The first time I went ballistic—when our friends had the nerve to cancel our dinner plans because of a massive snowstorm—my husband just stood there in the corner, looking like he had just watched me tear the head off a chicken with my bare hands. My mother would have blown me off and walked away, or even engaged in the action if the mood permitted, but my husband didn't have the foggiest idea how to handle it. It all seemed so childish and pointless to a man who didn't even raise his voice—in fear or anger—when his car once slid off the road on a patch of ice in the middle of a densely wooded area.

The first few times I had an angry outburst, Scott remained calm and either grabbed the car keys and went for a drive or excused himself to another part of the house. Although he didn't react at first, he didn't get over it right away either, even after I apologized and tried to make amends. He stayed quiet for the rest of the day and avoided talking to me any more than necessary.

But eventually, after living through too many of my "episodes," something about my anger brought out the anger in him, and he learned to fire back.

When he yelled back and fed me sarcasm, it made everything worse, and all he did was pour gasoline on what was already a raging inferno. That was how we started having screaming matches.

He told me I was crazy, that he didn't care if we stayed together or not. One time, when I had been at home unable to go any-where for nearly a month after my car accident, I was on edge from being cooped up in the house for so long. Neither of us can remember what sparked the argument, but we both re-member the angry, vulgar words that Scott shot back. It was not a manic episode, but Scott was programmed by then to expect the worst and react to it out of self-defense.

When I was in a depression, Scott handled that much better. Even with all the animosity in the house, Scott had mercy on me when I was sad. My tears melted him, and he came to my rescue like a true superhero. I know that part of what held us together was my need to be cared for and his need to care for me. That may sound so 1950-ish, and many modern-day therapists would disapprove of such sentiment, but it is what the "for better or for worse" part of the marriage vows are all about. He knew he was designed to comfort me, and I knew I was designed to be comforted by him. But it was hard staying in those roles, and after turning to my husband for support a few times, I stopped going to him. I felt like a giant burden to him when I was in a downward spiral.

People who don't have to live with depression (or who are in denial about their own) go out of their way to "fix" things. In my experience, the idea is either to exhaust oneself by trying to cheer the depressed person up (which is usually impossible, since mood is not the cause of the chemical imbalance, the chemical imbalance is the cause of the mood), or to shake them and snap 'em out of it. How many times have you heard people say, "I think so-and-so could pull himself up by his bootstraps and snap out of it if he wanted to"? The first idea that it's possible to cheer a clinically depressed person up is seldom ever possible, and the second idea that depression sufferers just need to "get over it" is ignorant. I don't particularly want to deal with either false notion, so I pull away and try to tough it out on my own. No, my husband never implied either to me, but I knew he couldn't understand what I was going through. I assumed, however wrongly, that he was thinking all of those things.

For a long time I told nobody how I felt, or I called my friend in Georgia, or I confided in a coworker that things were not going well, but I said nothing at home. He knew when I was depressed—it was obvious. But I didn't want to talk to him about it. He has always held up his end of the bargain, trying to reach out to me in my sorrow. One of my greatest sins as a wife is that I haven't always reached back.

Peace at Last

For almost two years now, an older Christian woman has mentored me. I have always felt comfortable sharing my heart with her, and she knows she has permission to be brutally honest with me whenever necessary, even though sometimes I give her a hard time about it! Almost from day one, as soon as I told her the sad state of my marriage, she encouraged me to seek professional help again and stop trying to go it alone. I humored her but never took any action until that night in February when Scott and I had to make a final decision about our future. I vowed to him I would get healthy. I may always be bipolar, but I can take steps to make things better, and it's not fair that my husband had to put up with unnecessary stress that could have been alleviated a long time ago.

One of the first things I did after we decided to stay together was that I went to see a psychologist. She asked me about my family history and took an inventory of my symptoms. I told her how frustrated I was by my inability to fall asleep and stay asleep. I described to her how my ups and downs made the average woman's monthly mood swings look like a ride at Disney World, and I shared how much of a toll it had taken on my marriage. After two hours of answering questions, she closed the cover of her diagnostic manual and said, "Yup, it sounds like you're bipolar!"

Like I said, I didn't believe her at first, because I was under the impression that mania always meant euphoria. But after she described Bipolar 2 to me, it made sense, and I knew I had found some answers. I always knew I had depression, but I also knew there was more to it than that. Having answers meant having hope, and having hope meant finding some direction. Not long after that appointment, I started seeing a doctor who prescribed me Lithium, a mood-stabilizing drug that leveled me out and, best of all, helped me get some much-needed sleep.

I can't explain how much better I feel and how much happier my marriage is now. My husband tells people that I'm "a delight to live with," which is much nicer than overhearing him on the phone saying, "I don't know how much longer I can live like this!" I still get mad sometimes—I'm a human being. And I'm a woman, which means every so often I'm prone to grouchiness, which has nothing to do with BP. My husband has a nickname for me when I am grouchy: Grumpopotamus. Being the sweet-heart that Scott is, he tells me that he thinks the changes in me came directly from God doing a work in my heart, not so much the counseling or the medication. I say it was a combination of both. God certainly sent me to the right people at the right time, no matter how you choose to look at it.

Yes, I have Bipolar Disorder, and yes, I take medication, but I don't want to skip out on driving home this point: I was an angry person. I was angry about my past, angry that I had let my past seep into my adulthood, and angry that my marriage was unhealthy. Medication cleared my head enough for me to realize and accept this, and counseling has helped me deal with it.

If you're a married person who struggles with anger, then you understand the frustration of not being able to win, no matter what you do. If your spouse tries to be comforting and sooth-ing, you get angry because you feel like they're blowing you off or minimizing your anger. If they fight back, you get angry because you can't believe they have the nerve to engage with you. If they simply walk away, you fault them for being a wimp who doesn't want to face you. But somewhere in the mix, there is a lesser evil. The key is finding the lesser evil and coming to an agreement with your spouse over how you are going to utilize that.

For example, as illustrated above, when I'm angry, I'm not easy to please. Any reaction is bound to tick me off—*initially*. But as it turned out, when my husband responded to me in love—acknowledging that I was angry and actually hugging me (which is a lot like willingly stepping into a minefield, I have to admit)—while I got angrier at first, I eventually couldn't deny that he was making a strong effort and that I was the one acting like a jerk. His love and physical touch defused my rage, which goes along with the theme of 1 Peter 4:8, "Above all, love each other deeply, because love covers over a multitude of sins." In my case, it was to be taken literally!

My husband and I have had many conversations about this very topic. He knows that walking away from me or (worse yet) getting in the car to leave is like fanning an open flame. And arguing back just opens the door to more hurtful words on both sides. It is not easy to wrap your arms around someone who is verbally attacking you (or physically attacking inanimate objects), but my husband knows this is the most painless way of dealing with me. Does he always do it? No. He's human. It's still easier to walk away or lash out. But his efforts have made a big difference in our home. What he does for me is the essence of selflessness. It's extremely important that you and your spouse know how to deal with anger issues. If you can't work it out on your own, just between the two of you, don't be afraid to seek help. We did, and we haven't regretted it for a minute.

I still get angry when I spend too much time dwelling on who I used to be, but there are more good times than bad ones now. When I know that I am cycling (I can always tell), I try to give people fair warning, especially my husband. Still, even when I am cycling, I am able to control myself and not go to extremes as much as I used to. It is very rare that I become so angry I get enraged, and it is also very rare that I contemplate harming myself anymore. And the fact that I was able to write this book, after a lifetime of not being able to finish anything I started, was a major victory for me.

Being a Good Spouse Under Bad Circumstances

Shortly after I conducted the Internet survey for the premarital counseling article I was writing, I conducted a survey about the impact mental illness has on marriages. I got some very honest and moving responses, and both Scott and I could relate to all of them.

Possibly the most important response I received came from a woman my age whose marriage had ended in divorce due to her struggles with depression:

> If you suspect something may be wrong, DO NOT ignore it or discount it. I have to live every day for the rest of my life knowing that I destroyed our marriage and that it could have easily been prevented. I'm not huge on the psychosocial sci-ences, but some things are just too important to ignore. Don't expect to fully understand how they are feeling; sometimes it's just not possible ... Reassure them with your love. Don't withhold yourself from them because you don't understand. That was one of our downfalls. James didn't understand what I was going through so he withdrew from me, which just made it worse. Remain committed, no matter what. Even if you don't "feel" love for them, your job as their spouse is to

show them God's love. So at the times when it's hardest to love them, just resolve to show them God's love. And never stop praying for them.

I couldn't have said it better myself.

You can't expect your spouse to understand your emotional problems if he doesn't have them himself. You have to really experience it to "get it." But you have to work toward keeping an open line of communication and be willing to explain your illness to your spouse. After all, he can't help you if he doesn't know what he's dealing with.

Those lines of communication flung open wide after we started to realize that it wasn't just my problem, or just his problem, but a problem that we shared. Part of being "one" means dually carrying each other's burdens.

Reflections:

1. If a husband and wife are considered "one" in God's eyes, then how do you think something like mental illness, if not confronted and treated, might affect your mate?

2. What sorts of things can a spouse do to help their mate face up to their illness? How should they respond to angry outbursts, tears, and overall frustration?

3. How do you think unresolved issues from the past impact a person with mental illness?

4. What can a spouse with mental illness do to help their mate understand and survive the turmoil that sometimes goes with it?

5. What are some things a spouse should not do in handling a mate with mental illness?

Scriptures:

Ephesians 4:26-27
"In your anger, do not sin": Do not let the sun go down while you are still angry, and do not give the devil a foothold.

Proverbs 18:21
The tongue has the power of life and death.

Luke 4:18
He has anointed me to preach good news to the poor. He has sent me to proclaim freedom for the prisoners and recovery of sight for the blind, to release the oppressed.

Chapter Seven

Final Thoughts

This is the house of empty rooms
This is the home of broken hearts
Where we came together
Where we moved apart
Behind doors of many stories
In the shadows of doubt
In this house of empty rooms
We could not work things out

This is the house of wandering souls
Looking for the life they knew
And I am unsettled
Finding traces of you
The halls have seen our anger
The windows knew our doubt
And the walls of many pictures
May never let us out

This is the house of empty rooms
With our names still carved in wood
I'd do it all over
If only I could
Behind doors of many stories
In the shadows of doubt
In this house of empty rooms
How I prayed we'd work things out

When I was almost certain that Scott and I were going to divorce, I flopped down on my bed one night with a pen and notebook and scribbled out this poem. It was meant to be a song, and I can still hear the tune to it in my head, but I never actually pulled out my guitar and composed anything because it would have been too painful. I stuck it in a manila folder with the rest of my poems and song lyrics and didn't give it much thought until I started writing this final chapter. Nothing else could quite describe the resignation I was feeling at that period in my life.

I don't know how marriages last without God. I have never believed in luck, but that's the only thing I can think of. When everything falls out from under you, and your love for one another has faded, and you start wondering if life would be easier if you lived it apart, where do you turn? Without God, there is no "cord of three strands" (Eccles. 4:12). It's just two partners against the world, and when they unravel, all is lost. When Scott and I couldn't stand it anymore and throwing in the towel seemed like the best idea, God still had a firm grip on us. No matter how hard things got, we had an awareness of Him and His love for us. We believed deep down, beneath the bitterness and sense of loss, that God had not joined us together only to watch us be destroyed. But we had to make the effort. In the end, you have to save yourself. I'll probably get a lot of letters from angry readers about that one, but it's the truth.

Think about it. God's arms are always outstretched and reaching for you. The words of Luke 11:9 tell us to, "Ask and it will be given to you; seek and you will find; knock and the door will be opened to you." You're always welcome ... but you must ask, seek, and knock. It's a lot like a well-known analogy about a man caught on the roof of his house in a flood when someone in a raft floats up. The guy in the raft throws him a rope and tells him to grab on, but the man on the roof refuses. "I don't need your help," he says. "I know God is going to save me!" The raft floats away, and a little while later a helicopter hovers overhead and lowers a ladder for the man to climb up. But again the man refuses to climb the ladder because he says he knows God is going to help him. Well, eventually the man succumbs to the rising water and dies, and when he gets to heaven, he asks God, "Lord, I believed you were going to save me! Why didn't you ever come for me?" And the Lord tells him, "I did come for you! I sent you a raft and a helicopter, but you turned them away!"

The same is true of marriage. God is that third and most stable strand in your cord of three, but when you become unraveled, you have to hang on by that final thread and allow the healing to begin.

We are not living in a marriage-friendly world. It's one in which TV shows are produced where couples are sent to a tropical island to see how long it takes for somebody to cheat. On other shows, complete strangers marry each other for fifteen minutes of fame … oh, and cash. When you turn on the radio, you hear songs that glorify casual sex, and the more partners you have, the cooler you are. We go into marriage with a lot of strikes against us and the weight of the world on our shoulders.

When I was growing up, many of my friends came from broken homes. It always sort of astonished my parents, who had been married forever even when I was a little girl, but broken homes seemed totally normal to me. It was what I was used to seeing around me. But now that I'm married myself, I realize that what we have here is a generation full of disillusioned, misguided young adults who grew up hearing (and seeing) that marriage was temporary and not really any more important than being boyfriend and girlfriend. They did not grow up hearing that marriage was a sacred covenant.

Nobody ever demonstrated to them what marriage was supposed to be like, so it shouldn't surprise anyone that half of all marriages end in divorce. I believe that marriage is a sacred covenant between a man, a woman, and their God and that it's a union that has to be cultivated. That is the very nature of marriage, is it not? It's two people coming together and saying, "I'm in this for the long haul, no matter what." Otherwise, what is the point of tying the knot at all? But many people don't see it that way anymore, and that also explains why so many couples are living together with no vows whatsoever. I think that's how many prefer it. They've lived through the heartbreak of their parents' divorce (or divorces), and they don't want to go through it themselves.

I can't fault them for any of this because I understand how difficult marriage is. I understand how it feels to want to run away and start life over again as a single person. It's especially no fun being a twentysomething newlywed with severe depression, a

chronically ill husband, no sex life, sometimes no job, sometimes
no money, to name just a few obstacles. When our marriage
was in its infancy stage, I looked at everything we were going through, and it all seemed insurmountable. Now I look at
everything we've been through, both proud and astounded that
we survived, and nothing else looks insurmountable anymore.
Whatever is up ahead, we'll find a way to put our shoulders to
the grind and plow through it together.

Is There a Case for Divorce?

When my husband and I were at the end of our rope, we both
got a lot of advice. We are blessed with good friends who love
us and want the best for us, and none of them would intention-
ally steer us wrong. I was stunned to find, however, that some of
the people in our lives who have always been the most vehe-
mently opposed to divorce suggested we take that exact route.
My own parents, who took Scott aside the day after we got
engaged and told him our family "doesn't believe in" divorce,
extended the invitation for me to leave and move back home
with them until I could get on my feet again. When you see
the people you deeply care about so unhappy, it's easy to make
exceptions to your own rules and standards because you want to
see them restored.

But I am forever grateful to the people who did not back down
from their belief that our marriage had potential and could be
healed with much prayer and elbow grease. One friend in particular fielded some pretty desperate-sounding phone calls from
me, literally pleading with her to accept that it wasn't going to
last. She said, and I quote, "Not a chance!" She also prayed with
me over the phone, encouraged me with in-depth emails, and
told me what she envisioned for our marriage down the line,
if we stuck it out. (She believed we would someday minister
to hurting couples—imagine that!) At times, I got furious with

her for being so immovable, but if she had ever told me, "You know, I've changed my mind. I think you should get divorced after all," it would have crushed my spirit. Even though I was frustrated with her for being so stubborn, I was grateful that she took a stand.

I was also helped by my best friend of more than thirteen years, who listened without judgment and offered very little advice. As I sat across from her in a Philadelphia Starbucks last summer, telling her that Scott and I were still struggling but I wanted to keep working at it, she was my sounding board, and her promise to be there for me no matter what I decided to do gave me a lot of comfort and freedom.

The intended message of this book is simple. Don't give up, don't give in, and don't throw in the towel. If we can make it, so can you. You are never without hope as long as you have God in your corner. You can find love and intimacy where it appears your bonds have been all but destroyed. It won't be easy. It will be the hardest thing you've ever done, and sometimes you'll want to burn your bridges, but hang on! I promise you, healing can be yours. This book was designed to offer encouragement, but I know not every marriage will stay intact, and it would be ignorant of me to ignore the topic.

Matthew 19:8-9 gives us the circumstances under which God believes divorce is acceptable: "Jesus replied, 'Moses permitted you to divorce your wives because your hearts were hard. But it was not this way from the beginning.' I tell you that anyone who divorces his wife, except for marital unfaithfulness, and marries another woman commits adultery."

This scripture does not instruct couples that they necessarily should divorce under these circumstances; it merely offers it as an option. However, many relationships can and do survive unfaithfulness. My good friend Ben Wilson and his wife, Ann, have started a ministry based out of Littleton, Colorado, called Marriages Restored (*www.marriagesrestored.com*). The Wilsons survived Ann's long-time affair, and their marriage was radically healed and transformed by God. They now counsel other married couples and conduct seminars and workshops about how to heal from infidelity.

There are topics I didn't cover in this book because (fortunately) I have not had to deal with them in my marriage. There has not been physical abuse, for example. I do not fear for my life, or for the lives of my children. As I wrote at the beginning of the book, I did my share of partying early on, but we have not had to contend with rampant addictions in our marriage, so we have no experience in living with an alcoholic or a drug-abusing spouse. I can concede to the fact that such situations are very extreme in nature and would easily crack the very foundation of any marriage.

I would never advise anyone to stay in a truly dangerous situation. No one should have to put up with physical abuse of any kind. Do I believe it's possible to find help and healing even for something as extreme as that? Yes, though I understand why that might not be a very popular answer.

I would also never fault anyone for getting a divorce. Regardless of my personal stance on the issue, it is definitely not the unforgivable sin. No one can ever know the whole truth behind what goes wrong in a broken marriage. There are two sides to every story, and usually those stories clash due to different perspectives and hard feelings. Couples that are in the process of divorcing need the love and support of friends, not their condemnation. I learned this the hard way twice.

Over the last several years, I have seen two of my friends go through divorces. Everyone involved got hurt as the general population picked apart their mistakes and missteps and placed the blame on the lesser-known spouses, without any real thought or logic behind it. One of those friends was a Christian known for touting morality and for the emphasis she placed on working on hurting relationships. In fact, she was one of the people who had encouraged me so strongly to make my marriage work. When I found out she was divorcing her husband, I was disappointed and angry. I told her she was a hypocrite and begged her to reconsider, but she had already made up her mind. Needless to say, we had words. I alienated her, and for months, we didn't talk. Finally, I called her and told her that while I didn't agree with her choice and probably never would, I shouldn't have attacked her without really knowing the facts. And even if I had, I should have expressed my concerns while adding that my love and friendship would remain a constant. Fortunately for me, she was very gracious and forgiving.

We need to guide couples toward healing, not divorce. We need to speak up and make it clear that we don't believe giving up is an option. But then we also need to love those who choose it anyway, because none of us can accurately judge another person's heart ... especially when it is wounded and hurting. Broken couples need to know that God hates divorce (Mal. 2:16), but He loves His children. It's our job to demonstrate that love.

What It Will Take to Patch the Holes

It's understandable and almost expected that the divorce rate is so high among the mainstream, but what is so disturbing is that the divorce rate within the Church is higher than in the mainstream! According to the Barna Research Group, the divorce rate among born-again Christians is higher than it is among even atheists and agnostics.[2] According to George Barna, president and founder of Barna Research Group, a lack of support seems to be the culprit.

> While it may be alarming to discover that born again Christians are more likely than others to experience a divorce, that pattern has been in place for quite some time. Even more disturbing, perhaps, is that when those individuals experience a divorce, many of them feel their community of faith provides rejection rather than support and healing. But the research also raises questions regarding the effectiveness of how churches minister to families. The ultimate responsibility for a marriage belongs to the husband and wife, but the high incidence of divorce within the Christian community challenges the idea that churches provide truly practical and life-changing support for marriages.

In chapter 5, I referred to a premarital counseling article I wrote in which I created a random Internet survey taken by several hundred couples. Well, those couples not only claimed finances as their biggest stressor, but they all agreed on one other thing—married couples desperately need the support of their church families, but help is not always easy to find. I asked my survey-takers if they thought churches provided enough help, and many said they did not:

> *We think churches start too late. You're not going to counteract twenty to twenty-five years of bad habits and unrealistic expectations with sixteen hours of meeting with a semi-stranger. Churches should integrate preparation for marriage into the teaching of young people from a very early age, and*

they should help parents purposefully prepare their children for marriage.

I felt that my church did not have that much support for pre-marital, and I have not seen any support in my current church for newlyweds.

I also asked them what they thought was a good way to reduce the divorce rate and once again make marriage a lifelong, sacred union:

Stop marrying unprepared couples! If they disagree on whether to have children, what faith to raise children in, are abusive or addicted to sex or substances, they should not marry until that issue has been resolved. Take a look at the factors that contribute to divorce and start weeding those out, or offer programs with proven effectiveness rates and require troubled couples to take them.

People need to stop thinking that life is all about having fun and start thinking in terms of service and self-giving. (Note from Julie: I'm all in favor of fun, as long as we include self-giving!)

I think it's primarily the responsibility of the father/husband. Fathers are responsible to love, cherish, and uplift their wives and lead a vibrant marriage relationship as an example for their children. They should love and nurture their daughters so they feel confident as women and don't feel the need to seek random male approval. And of equal importance to the first two, they must train their sons to be good men, honoring women as persons and not as possessions or just playmates. These sons would then grow up to respect most women, and love and cherish one. And the cycle would begin all over again …

Read C.S. Lewis' Mere Christianity *where he says marriage isn't about mere feelings. There is a dimension of marriage that is like faith, a vow that is constant regardless of the ebb and flow of emotion. Our media images of romance stress spontaneity over fidelity. Churches need to preach about this and offer a better message.*

Training on communication for all stages of marriage. Help in working on discussion and negotiation skills. Make counseling less of a stigma for men.

These are just a few examples of what other couples had to say, but everyone had excellent ideas. I agree with all of the ideas listed above. A solid marriage requires faith over feelings (because, remember, feelings follow actions, not the other way around) and a firm commitment to ride the waves of life as they come.

Since I started writing this book, I have spoken with many hurting couples, and many of them did not seek support until their marriage was on the rocks. My husband and I made the same mistake, and I can't help but wonder how many problems might have been alleviated if we had taken the time to find fellowship early on. We now meet with another couple once a week for fun and fellowship. Just like us, they were on the verge of destruction before they sought help. The four of us agree the journey would have been significantly less bumpy had we stuck together in the first place.

Marriages also need prayer, which is in the same category as fellowship. But I'm not just talking about praying for and with friends, though that is also critical. You've probably heard the saying, "The couple that prays together stays together." It's more than a cute rhyme; it's a very solid truth. In this hedonistic society, we associate sex with being the peak of intimacy, but I would argue that prayer is the ultimate intimacy. There is something amazingly powerful about a married couple falling on their knees together before the Lord. It is a supernatural intimacy. Prayer is the glue that holds a couple together, not sex. It is the responsibility of the Church to create avenues for fellowship and to provide sound biblical teaching on the importance of prayer within a marriage.

It is also the Church's responsibility to shift the focus away from saving doomed marriages (I said shift the focus away, not do away with) to preventing their demise from the moment a man and a woman say, "I do."

Parting Words

I covered a lot of ground in this book, yet it was obviously impossible to cover everything that needs to be talked about. I am an imperfect woman, and I am married to an imperfect man. I am not a psychologist; neither is he. My life and my marriage underwent a radical transformation. God brought me from death to life, and that's no exaggeration. In the aftermath, I felt called to share my experiences with others, in the hopes it might help people save their marriages, improve upon an already good marriage, or prepare engaged couples for the fact that sometimes reality is just no fun!

There are no perfect marriages, but I am convinced that when the involved parties are devoted to God, there are no hopeless ones either. I can tell you with full confidence that Scott and I are now happy together and are on the road to full recovery. There is mutual respect where there was once anger and neglect. We are affectionate and loving, and we laugh a lot. My husband is my best friend, and if I were given the choice to spend a weekend with anyone in the world, I would choose

Scott, hands down. We are each other's world.

My hope is that whatever state you currently find your marriage in—good, bad, or ugly—you will let God be the strongest strand in your cord of three. I pray that you will be able to trust Him enough to rescue you if you're lost, nurture you if you're stable, and strengthen you for the long road ahead—the long road you'll be traveling *together.*

Till death do you part.

Reflections:

1. What information or help could you have received before you got married that would have better prepared you for the road ahead? How might you help other couples (or suggest to your church that they help other couples) receive that help early on?

2. In this chapter, you read the author's thoughts on why the divorce rate is so high. What are your opinions on why divorce is so prevalent?

3. What, in your opinion, is the most important thing the Church can do to protect marriages?

4. What sorts of things can an engaged or newlywed couple do to make sure they have a healthy, lifelong relationship?

5. What is the greatest challenge facing your marriage?

Scriptures:

James 1:4
Perseverance must finish its work so that you may be mature and complete, not lacking anything.

1 Corinthians 10:13
And God is faithful; he will not let you be tempted beyond what you can bear. When you are tempted, he will provide a way out so that you can stand up under it.

Julie Anne Fidler
author

Julie Anne Fidler's work has appeared in various publications, including the RELEVANT Leader, RELEVANT Magazine, and CMCentral. She is creative works editor at *Infuze* magazine (*www.infuzemag.com*) and is a freelance feature writer for a local weekly newspaper. She lives in Pennsylvania, where she also works with teenage mothers. She has been married to her best friend, Scott, for four and a half years. You can contact her via email: JAFid79@aol.com, or visit her blog: *www.fidlerontheroof. blogspot.com*.

Citations

1. For more information, see *http://www.nimh.nih.gov/publicat/bipolar.cfm#bp1*, accessed December 30, 2004.

2. "U.S. Divorce Rates: For various faith groups, age groups, & geographic areas," Religioustolerance.org, *http://www.religioustolerance.org/chr_dira.htm*, accessed January 2, 2005.

[RELEVANTBOOKS]

FOR MORE INFORMATION ABOUT OTHER RELEVANT BOOKS,

check out *www.relevantbooks.com*.